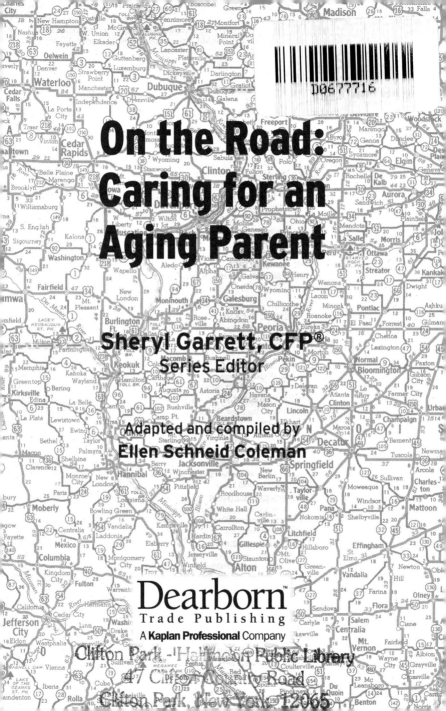

On the Road: Caring for an Aging Parent

Sheryl Garrett, CFP®
Series Editor

Adapted and compiled by
Ellen Schneid Coleman

Dearborn™
Trade Publishing
A **Kaplan Professional** Company

This publication is designed to provide accurate and authoritative information in regard to the subject matter covered. It is sold with the understanding that the publisher is not engaged in rendering legal, accounting, or other professional service. If legal advice or other expert assistance is required, the services of a competent professional person should be sought.

President, Dearborn Publishing: Roy Lipner
Vice President and Publisher: Cynthia A. Zigmund
Senior Acquisitions Editor: Mary B. Good
Cover Design: Design Solutions

Published by Dearborn Trade Publishing
A Kaplan Professional Company

A Stonesong Press Book

Project Manager: Ellen Schneid Coleman
Interior Design: Brad Walrod/High Text Graphics, Inc.

Printed in the United States of America

06 07 08   10 9 8 7 6 5 4 3 2 1

Library of Congress Cataloging-in-Publication Data
Caring for an aging parent/edited by Sheryl Garrett; adapted and compiled by Ellen Schneid Coleman.
    p.   cm.—(On the road)
  Includes index.
  ISBN 1-4195-0043-0 (5 × 7.375 pbk.)
  1. Aging parents—United States.   2. Finance, Personal—United States.
3. Aging parents—Caring—United States.   I. Garrett, Sheryl.   II. Coleman, Ellen Schneid.   III. On the road (Chicago, Ill.)
HQ1063.6.C365 2006
362.6'0973—dc22   2005021737

Dearborn Trade books are available at special quantity discounts to use for sales promotions, employee premiums, or educational purposes. Please call our Special Sales Department to order or for more information at 800-621-9621, ext. 4444, e-mail trade@dearborn.com, or write to Dearborn Trade Publishing, 30 South Wacker Drive, Suite 2500, Chicago, IL 60606-7481.

1748

Contents

Introduction

On the Road: Caring for an Aging Parent is part of a new series of books from Dearborn Trade Publishing intended to help you deal with the financial issues, problems, and decisions concerning specific life events. The decisions you will be called up to make when you're faced with caring for an aging parent are obviously very different from the decisions you have to make about anything else.

With advances in medical science and increases in longevity, it is not uncommon to see people living into their 90s and beyond. As a result, more and more of us will need to participate in the care of an aging parent. As the baby boomers age, so, too, do their parents. The good news is that most of our parents will be living longer, healthier, more active, and productive lives. At some point, however, we may all be called upon to lend a hand. If that day arrives, it may be scary and upsetting if we are not prepared for it. But we can prepare for it, and we can help our parents prepare for it.

Many books address the multitude of emotional issues parents, children, and other family members have to consider when they undertake this responsibility. Few address the myriad financial and legal issues that accompany this highly emotional subject. It is our aim in *On the Road: Caring for an Aging Parent* to fill that gap.

We have designed this book for those of you who are about to or already are caring for a parent (some of you may even be caring for two), and it is also for those who are thinking about the future. The ideal situation would be for you and your parents to plan in advance for the possibility together. In that way, you and they would discuss their retirement plans, for example, with an eye toward future possibilities. The same would be true of health care and other issues that we face as we age.

Financial planning shouldn't be intimidating. So we've created these books to take away the terror. *On the Road* books are set up like travel guides to help you make the best financial decisions at each stage of your life—in this case, also at an important stage in your parents' lives. This book addresses these vital issues:

▶ knowing where mom has tucked away important papers; for example, medical records, bank books, stock records and certificates, life insurance policies; or

▶ who is dad's lawyer, cardiologist, broker and how do you get in touch with them;

▶ where should your mother live once she has retired; if she chooses to move to another state how will she be taken care of in the event she falls ill and needs long-term care;

▶ what benefits is dad entitled to from his company? what about the company before that? and before that? how about benefits from the state or federal government? has he applied for them?

▶ what assets do they have to retire on; will they last?

▶ are their estate plans up-to-date; do you know what kind of funeral they want; does someone have a medical power of attorney? what about a financial power of attorney?

These financial and legal decisions are part of your parents' life's journey, but they may also be part of yours. For this reason, we've made them easy to navigate, with lots of helpful "Roadmaps" (charts and tables of financial information to help you with each issue or decision that comes up) and "Tollbooths" that help you calculate your expenses or savings, as well as "Hazard" signs that caution you on money pitfalls to watch out for. We've included "What to Pack" so that you'll know what forms or other information you or your parents will need along the road.

Finally, the end of the book includes an "Itinerary," a recap of all the key actions you and your parents should take—all of which are discussed in detail in the five chapters of this book. At the end we have included a list of other books and resources you could turn to if you want more in-depth information on estate planning or life insurance, retirement planning, and healthcare options.

We hope you, together with your parents, find this "travel" guide offers peace of mind as you map the route. So let's get started on the road: the light is green, there are many options before you, let's explore them!

Where Are You Now?

Facing the Future Together

Getting older isn't what it once was. A person who is 65 today has an excellent chance to reach 85 (see Roadmap 1.1), and with medical advances may live even longer, healthier lives. Many seniors will never require the assistance of their children for financial, health, or other reasons. Many of them will have prepared for all eventualities, and will live happy, healthy, productive, and comfortable lives—enjoying the benefits and new experiences that come with proper planning. If your parents are like these, and many are, caring for them may simply mean being aware, pitching in when and if necessary, and helping them make the transitions as needed.

Other parents, for a variety of reasons, may need our help—most often as a result of poor health, insufficient finances or inexperience dealing with financial matters, or the loss of a spouse. In such cases, the emotional trauma of caring for an aging parent may be one of the hardest things you will have to face. As each succeeding generation lives longer and longer, more and more of us will have to consider this situation.

Some of us may have to deal with an aging parent's needs even as we are raising our own children. Many of us will have to confront the challenge after the loss of one parent. Typically, when both parents are alive, they care for one another, and their children have less need to be involved

Roadmap 1.1

IRS Life Expectancy Tables

Your parent's age	# of yrs the IRS expects your parent to live	Your parent's age	# of yrs the IRS expects your parent to live	Your parent's age	# of yrs the IRS expects your parent to live
65	21.0	81	9.7	97	3.6
66	20.2	82	9.1	98	3.4
67	19.4	83	8.6	99	3.1
68	18.6	84	8.1	100	2.9
69	17.8	85	7.6	101	2.7
70	17.0	86	7.1	102	2.5
71	16.3	87	6.7	103	2.3
72	15.5	88	6.3	104	2.1
73	14.8	89	5.9	105	1.9
74	14.1	90	5.5	106	1.7
75	13.4	91	5.2	107	1.5
76	12.7	92	4.9	108	1.4
77	12.1	93	4.6	109	1.2
78	11.4	94	4.3	110	1.1
79	10.8	95	4.1	111	
80	10.2	96	3.8	and over	1.0

Source: IRS 2004 Publication 590

in their everyday affairs like the state of their finances, health, and, in some instances, leisure time.

It's our hope that you are reading this book before a crisis occurs. It makes it easier if you can plan ahead. Even if that's not the case, if it is at all possible, the best way to approach caring for a parent (and to relieve some of the anxiety you, your parent, and other family members may have) is to discuss the situation openly.

Whether you are reading this book because you are doing some advance thinking and planning or because you are faced with a pressing need or anything in between, you'll find the answers to many of your questions about finances, living arrangements, and healthcare, as well as estate planning, legal and other related issues. The good news is that in today's world, there are many options to fit the myriad different situations that may arise.

We'll begin this trip by showing you how to help or to assess your parent's current needs and what their requirements would be down the road. (For the most part, we are assuming that you are caring for only one parent, but, of course, this information could well apply to caring for both.)

Hazard!

Support for Caregivers

According to the National Alliance for Caregiving, caregivers spend an average of four and one-half years and almost 12 hours a week providing care. This can be emotionally and financially costly.

Care giving may be one of the most important roles you will undertake in your lifetime. Usually it is not an easy role, nor is it one for which most of us are prepared. Like most people, you may have questions about how to cope with your care receiver's illnesses or disability. If you have a job and are juggling several responsibilities or if your family member needs a lot of assistance, you may need help with care giving, too. Whether you are expecting to become a caregiver or have been thrust into the role overnight, it is useful to know where you can get information and help.

The enactment of the Older Americans Act Amendments of 2000 (Public Law 106-501) established an important program, the National Family Caregiver Support Program (NFCSP). The program was developed by the Administration on Aging (AoA) of the U.S. Department of Health and Human Services (HHS). Visit: http://www.aoa.gov/prof/aoaprog/caregiver/caregiver.asp for helpful information on topics ranging from costs of care giving to tips on surviving the stresses you may experience.

▶ Travel Plans: Getting a Grip on Your Parent's Current Needs

Do you know how much money your mom has, where dad put his will—for that matter do you know if he even has an up-to-date will? What about your parents' medical insurance? And have they made plans for where they want to live? It's important that you know the answers to these questions and a host of other questions much in advance.

If possible, work with your parent to fill out Roadmap 1.2. Tip: It's worth taking the time to get organized before you begin. The time commitment will be minimal compared to the return you and your parent will earn from getting a handle on his or her finances.

The best way to get started is to set up a filing system separate from your own files. In addition to setting up a separate file for each of the categories described in the Recordkeeping Worksheet (Roadmap 1.2), it is crucial to note on the worksheet where all the important documents of your parents are located. You need to know other details such as account numbers and the names of brokers, insurance agents, and other people who know about their accounts.

Many a widow tells the story of how she was thrown into total financial chaos when her husband died suddenly and all the records were scattered throughout the house. The same will be true for you if you don't make sure your mom is organized. She may know where everything is, but in an emergency, you probably won't—unless, of course, you've gone through this exercise. The time you spend now will be worth it down the road apiece.

Roadmap 1.2, then, is a worksheet that consolidates all of your parent's important data in one place. You should organize your filing system using the exact same categories, which are arranged alphabetically. As you'll see, we've included personal information about both parents. Even if one parent is deceased, you may need this information when filing for Social Security, veteran's, pension, and other benefits.

Roadmap 1.2

Recordkeeping Worksheet

1. Personal Information

Your Name _____
Spouse's Name _____
Address _____
Home Telephone _____
Work Telephone/FAX _____
Date, Place of Birth _____
Birth Certificate Location _____
Social Security Number _____
Marital Status _____

Your Father's Name _____
Spouse's Name _____
Address _____
Home Telephone _____
Work Telephone/FAX _____
Date, Place of Birth _____
Birth Certificate Location _____
Social Security Number _____
Marital Status _____

Your Mother's Name _____
Spouse's Name _____
Address _____
Home Telephone _____
Work Telephone/FAX _____
Date, Place of Birth _____
Birth Certificate Location _____
Social Security Number _____
Marital Status _____

Your Sibling's Name(s) _____
Spouse's Name _____
Address _____
Home Telephone _____
Work Telephone/FAX _____
Date, Place of Birth _____
Birth Certificate Location _____
Social Security Number _____
Marital Status _____

Roadmap 1.2 (continued)

Recordkeeping Worksheet

Your Child's Name(s) _____
Spouse's Name _____
Address _____
Home Telephone _____
Work Telephone/FAX _____
Date, Place of Birth _____
Birth Certificate Location _____
Social Security Number _____
Marital Status _____

Sibling's Child's Name(s) _____
Spouse's Name _____
Address _____
Home Telephone _____
Work Telephone/FAX _____
Date, Place of Birth _____
Birth Certificate Location _____
Social Security Number _____
Marital Status _____

2. Professional Contacts
Accountant _____
Address _____
Telephone/FAX _____
Assistant's Name _____

Attorney _____
Address _____
Telephone/FAX _____
Assistant's Name _____

Banker _____
Address _____
Telephone/FAX _____
Assistant's Name _____

Dentist _____
Address _____
Telephone/FAX _____
Assistant's Name _____

Employee Benefits Counselor

Address _____

Telephone/FAX _____

Assistant's Name _____

Executor of Estate

Address _____

Telephone/FAX _____

Assistant's Name _____

Financial Planner

Address _____

Telephone/FAX _____

Assistant's Name _____

Insurance Agent (auto)

Address _____

Telephone/FAX _____

Assistant's Name _____

Insurance Agent (health)

Address _____

Telephone/FAX _____

Assistant's Name _____

Insurance Agent (home)

Address _____

Telephone/FAX _____

Assistant's Name _____

Insurance Agent (life)

Address _____

Telephone/FAX _____

Assistant's Name _____

Investment Manager

Address _____

Telephone/FAX _____

Assistant's Name _____

Physician

Address _____

Telephone/FAX _____

Assistant's Name _____

Priest/Rabbi/Minister

Address _____

Telephone/FAX _____

Assistant's Name _____

Recordkeeping Worksheet

Stockbroker _____
Address _____
Telephone/FAX _____
Assistant's Name _____

Trust Officer _____
Address _____
Telephone/FAX _____
Assistant's Name _____

Other _____
Address _____
Telephone/FAX _____
Assistant's Name _____

Other _____
Address _____
Telephone/FAX _____
Assistant's Name _____

3. Financial Accounts

Banking Records (CDs, checking, credit union, savings)

Name of Institution	Type of Account	Account Number	Location of Documents
_____	_____	_____	_____
_____	_____	_____	_____
_____	_____	_____	_____
_____	_____	_____	_____
_____	_____	_____	_____

Bonds (corporate, municipal, Treasury bonds)

Issuer	# of Bonds	Due Date	Location of Documents
_____	_____	_____	_____
_____	_____	_____	_____
_____	_____	_____	_____
_____	_____	_____	_____

Business Ownership

Name of Business	Type of Business	% Owned	Other Partners	Location of Documents
_____	_____	_____	_____	_____
_____	_____	_____	_____	_____

Children's Accounts

Child's Name	Trustee	Type of Account or Trust	Location of Funds
_____	_____	_____	_____
_____	_____	_____	_____
_____	_____	_____	_____

Debts (auto, credit card, education, mortgage)

Type of Loan	Name of Institution	Account Number	Amount Due	Monthly Payment
_____	_____	_____	_____	_____
_____	_____	_____	_____	_____
_____	_____	_____	_____	_____
_____	_____	_____	_____	_____

Employee Benefit and Retirement Plans (401(k), IRA, Keogh plans, pension plans, profit-sharing plans, stock purchase plans)

Type of Plan	Who Is Covered	Trustee	$ Value of Plan	Beneficiary(ies)
_____	_____	_____	_____	_____
_____	_____	_____	_____	_____
_____	_____	_____	_____	_____

Insurance Policies (auto, health, home, life insurance)

Type of Policy	Insures Who or What	Name of Company	Account Number	Location of Documents
_____	_____	_____	_____	_____
_____	_____	_____	_____	_____
_____	_____	_____	_____	_____
_____	_____	_____	_____	_____
_____	_____	_____	_____	_____

Mutual Funds

Type of Account	Name of Company	Account Number	Location of Documents
_____	_____	_____	_____
_____	_____	_____	_____
_____	_____	_____	_____

Real Estate

Type of Property	Location of Property	Date Purchased	Purchase Price $ Plus Cost of Improvements	Location of Documents
_____	_____	_____	_____	_____
_____	_____	_____	_____	_____
_____	_____	_____	_____	_____

Recordkeeping Worksheet

Safe-Deposit Boxes

Depository Bank and Address	Primary and Secondary Owner of Assets	Person with Power of Attorney	Location of Contents List and Key
_____	_____		
_____	_____	_____	_____
_____	_____		

Stocks

Type of Account	Name of Company	Account Number	Location of Documents
_____	_____	_____	_____
_____	_____	_____	_____
_____	_____	_____	_____
_____	_____	_____	_____
_____	_____	_____	_____

Tax Records

Persons Filing	Estimated Quarterly Payments	Location of Latest Tax Return and Records	Location of Previous Returns
_____	_____	_____	_____
_____	_____	_____	_____
_____	_____	_____	_____
_____	_____	_____	_____

Wills and Trust Documents (LPOAs, health and financial, living wills, funeral directives)

Family Member Covered	Attorney	Executor	Location of Documents
_____	_____	_____	_____
_____	_____	_____	_____
_____	_____	_____	_____
_____	_____	_____	_____

4. Other Important Papers

Location

Address _____

Appliance Instructions,
Guarantees, and
Warranties _____

Automobile Titles or
Lease Documents _____

Burial Plot Documentation _____

Citizenship Papers/
Passports _____

Club Membership
Records _____

Contracts _____

Credit Reports _____

Divorce Decrees _____

Educational Records and
Diplomas _____

Employment Records _____

Financial Records _____

Frequent Flier Account
Records _____

Health Care Proxy _____

Health Records _____

Home Improvement
Records _____

Inventories of Household
Goods _____

Jury Duty Records _____

Living Wills _____

Marriage Certificate _____

Medical Insurance Forms _____

Medicare Cards _____

Military Discharge Papers _____

Power of Attorney
Documents _____

Receipts for Major
Purchases _____

Religious Information _____

Rental Leases _____

Résumés _____

Social Security Cards and
Earnings Records _____

Utility Bills _____

Other (specify) _____

▶ Preparing for the Trip Ahead: Overview of Key Issues

If your parents planned for golden years most of their working lives, the transition which may have started in their 60s should be relatively smooth. Ideally, they will have accumulated enough capital through a combination of employee benefits plans and personal investments to produce enough income to live comfortably, no matter how old they get or what their future needs may be. They will have developed enough hobbies and other interests to fill in their free time, and will have thought about their housing options and, of course, done some estate planning.

Few people actually get around to mapping out all these aspects of their lives ahead of time. If your parent hasn't, it is important now to evaluate each aspect of your parent's personal finances so that you can understand where dad stands and what help he may need going forward.

Before Starting Out Assess the Terrain

Finances. We'll begin our journey with finances, since in many ways the rest of your parent's options may rest at least in part on them. At this point in his life, it is our hope that dad has amassed a significant amount of assets and paid off most, if not all, of his debts. He should be operating with a positive cash flow because many of the expenses of your earlier years, such as college tuition and buying everything from baby clothes to furniture, no longer apply. Assuming he has not yet retired, once he retires, he should receive income from Social Security, his company's pension plan (if any) or his own IRA or other retirement plan, and his personal investments.

If your parents have planned for retirement most of their working lives, they should know how much income they should be able to receive from pensions, IRAs, Keoghs, salary reduction plan, annuities, Social Security, and their personal investment portfolio. They should also have an estimate of their living expenses in retirement. In any case, it's advisable to work with them to reassess their budget every so often in order to adjust for changes in their financial situation and to realistically balance their expenses with their income. If your parents did not plan adequately for retirement, they will have a lot of catching up to do since they have run out of time to save and invest much or any money from salary. They must draw up a realistic budget based on the assets they have, the income those assets can generate, other income sources, such as pensions and Social Security, and their expenses. We will be reviewing these issues in detail in Chapter 2.

As dad moves through his 60s into his 70s, 80s and beyond, he should have a complete financial checkup every few years, at a minimum. (You may need to assist him as circumstances require.) The exercise will help keep you and him up to date with his financial situation.

Even if your parents have prepared for retirement, you may be faced with a situation where one parent is uninvolved with the family's finances. Some widows, for example, are ill-prepared to handle their personal finances alone. The same may be true for widowers if their wives took charge of the finances; however, it is often husbands who fail to involve their wives in the family's finances. If you are doing advance planning with both parents—and we hope you are—make sure they are both aware of all the financial issues.

On the other hand, if your mom or dad is in a muddle over day-to-day financial issues, you may have to scramble to reassemble their financial foundation. So much needs to be done, often when you and your parent are least able to cope. If one parent has recently died, you may be called upon to help the other parent collect on life insurance policies; establish a credit identity; work with estate lawyers, trustees, and probate courts; and assess an investment portfolio, among other things. These overwhelming circumstances can make a new widow(er) particularly vulnerable to misleading or self-serving advice from financial product salespeople presenting themselves as objective financial advisors.

In the next chapter, we'll walk you through what you need to do first, which is to help your parent get organized about finances, prepare a budget, and assess the options.

Housing. Probably the most important decision you can help your parent make is where they want to live (assuming that your parent is healthy enough for self-care). Most people remain in the homes they lived in while working, but many older people move to a warmer climate or a town that imposes less of a tax burden. While the lure of a warm and possibly faraway place and fresh start may be appealing in theory, it's important to help your parent think through such a decision carefully. In addition, of course, there are financial considerations; some parts of the country—the Midwest, for example—and the world are less expensive than others.

It can be difficult to put down new roots at a stage in life when mom or dad may just want to relax. They might also find that moving farther from their children, grandchildren, and close friends means that they see them less. Some older people, who may have friends in the new location or who are naturally gregarious and in good health or whose families do not live nearby, make this transition easily and thrive in their new setting. Others find it more difficult.

Another important consideration is that your parent will also have to replace an entire network of professionals. If your parent is not in good health, replacing doctors is something you should seriously consider before a move is made. We'll explore these and other issues and options that you and your parent should consider before making any major changes in lifestyle. We will explore these and other options in Chapter 3.

Health. It's important to know your family's medical history for two reasons: First and foremost, if your parent is unable to communicate that information to medical personnel, you should have it at your fingertips. Second, this information may help you and other family members with the diagnosis, early treatment, and, in some cases, prevention of hereditary medical conditions. Have your parent complete Roadmap 1.3. At the same time, it's a good idea to create a list of the medications (and their dosages) your parent takes (which should be updated when any changes are made) and a list of allergies, if any. You and your parent should keep a copy with you at all times.

Legal. Most Americans die without doing any kind of estate planning, even something as simple as executing a legally valid will. There are many explanations for why this is: Some simply never get around to it, because their lives are so busy, because estate planning doesn't sound like fun, or because they think that they will have plenty of time later to do their estate planning. Others mistakenly view estate planning as something that only rich people need to do. Then there are those who don't want to write a will or do any other kind of estate planning, because they are uncomfortable confronting the reality of their future death. We hope your parents fall into none of these categories and have developed an estate plan, which they update as needed. If not, we'll review the basics with you in Chapter 5.

There's another aspect of estate planning that you and your parent should also consider. Most people limit their concept of estate planning to writing a will, but there's much more to estate planning than just writing a will. For example, it also includes creating a living will and signing a medical power of attorney, among other things. These two, in particular, are something you should make certain your parent has considered.

Roadmap 1.3

Family Medical History

Have you or has any blood relative had any of the following? (Include your parent, the grandparents, sisters, brothers, uncles, aunts, and children.)

Yes No

— — Alcoholism

— — Alzheimer's disease

— — Arthritis

— — Birth defects (describe) _____

— — Blood disorder (describe, e.g., hemophilia, thalassemia)
_____

Cancer:

— — Breast cancer

— — Colon cancer

— — Melanoma

— — Other cancer (describe) _____

— — Chromosomal disorder (describe, e.g., Down's syndrome).

— — Collagen vascular disease (describe, e.g., lupus erythematosus, Raynaud's disease, rheumatoid arthritis, scleroderma)
_____

— — Cystic fibrosis

— — Diabetes

— — Endometriosis

— — Eczema

— — Epilepsy (seizures)

— — Glaucoma

— — Gout

— — Hay fever

Heart disease:

— — High blood pressure

— — High cholesterol

— — Other heart disorder (describe, e.g., Marfan's syndrome)
_____

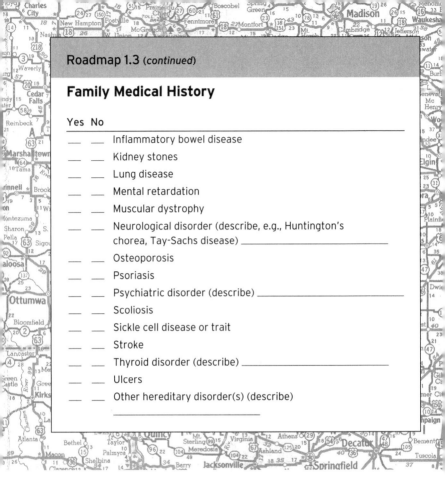

Roadmap 1.3 *(continued)*

Family Medical History

Yes	No	
—	—	Inflammatory bowel disease
—	—	Kidney stones
—	—	Lung disease
—	—	Mental retardation
—	—	Muscular dystrophy
—	—	Neurological disorder (describe, e.g., Huntington's chorea, Tay-Sachs disease) _____
—	—	Osteoporosis
—	—	Psoriasis
—	—	Psychiatric disorder (describe) _____
—	—	Scoliosis
—	—	Sickle cell disease or trait
—	—	Stroke
—	—	Thyroid disorder (describe) _____
—	—	Ulcers
—	—	Other hereditary disorder(s) (describe) _____

This will protect your mother or father if they become fatally ill or injured and can't make their own decisions or let the doctors know about the kinds of life-prolonging medical care and treatment they do want or do not want. Modern medicine and medical technology can keep them alive, sometimes indefinitely, irrespective of whether your parent wanted it or not. In Chapter 5, we'll also review some of the tools your parents can use to control their health and medical care when they can't speak for themselves. It also discusses tools they can use to ensure that their personal, business, financial, and legal affairs will be well managed if an illness or injury temporarily incapacitates them.

Talk about the Trip: Making Decisions Together

Initially this discussion may not be easy. Mom and dad are accustomed to taking care of themselves and are unused to sharing this information with their child. But it's important to tactfully broach these topics and start these discussions. Once they realize you are not prying or seeking to control, but are offering help, most parents recognize the importance of this planning and are willing to bring these issues—even their fears, if any—out into the open.

If you are wondering how to get started, think of your family as a small business and consider having a "family financial board meeting" on a regular fixed schedule. Indeed, this is a good time to state emphatically that if you have siblings, and it is possible to do so, involve them in the process of caring for your parents from the outset. Even if you will be the primary caregiver, it's important to have the support and agreement of other family members. Set up the ground rules so that your parents know this is a safe and supportive place and time to express their thoughts and questions.

Every parent's and family's needs are different, but here are some suggestions for how to productively use this family meeting time:

► Review your goals.
► Outline your parent(s)' spending choices and decisions.
► Find creative ways to resolve money shortages or to utilize extra funds.
► Work out logistics for who will handle certain responsibilities.
► Determine charitable giving, if appropriate.
► Be sure to acknowledge all the progress you have made as a "team" so far.

After a few months, or even weeks, you will begin to notice subtle changes everywhere—not just with the finances.

How Much Will This Trip Cost?

Budgeting for Now and the Future

Massive changes in society and advanced medical science and technology means that more people would live longer. Unlike earlier, people now live in retirement for longer periods of time. For example, advances in modern medicine commonly extend lives into the 80s, 90s, and even 100s.

In order to analyze your parent's financial condition, you must take stock of their finances, you need to know where they stand right now; that is, you must compute their net worth. Many seniors have prepared well for their retirement; others may not have been able to do so. In some cases, your parent may have this information at the fingertips; in others you'll be starting from scratch. In this chapter, we'll run through the key things you and your mom or dad should know.

Throughout this book, we emphasize the importance of planning in advance. Some of the information in this chapter will be of interest to all or most readers. We really hope that these would never concern you, but should the need arise, you and your parent will be well prepared.

▶ How Far Can Your Parent Travel?

Calculating net worth is like weighing in before the championship fight. To find out what someone weighs (financially, that is), you add up the total value of what the person already owns, known as *assets,* and subtract the amount of debt they owe, known as *liabilities.* This bottom line is known as that person's *net worth.* It is a snapshot in time, good only for the moment you calculate it, so if there are changes in your mother's financial condition, be sure to update her net worth.

How Much Is in the Travel Fund? Determining What Your Parent Owns *and* Owes

By doing this exercise, you will be able to see clearly how mom or dad's assets and liabilities match (or mismatch). If you are in the advance planning mode, dad may still be working full- or part-time. If so, you may discover ways to increase his savings and investment assets. Or, if dad is no longer working, you may find he's got spending under control, and there's less cause for concern. On the other hand, if you may find he's doing all the wrong things, like increasing his debt and depleting his savings, this may be a signal for you to step in and help figure out ways to pay off the debt and help him create a budget he can live on (more about that later in this chapter).

While you will want to monitor mom's net worth once a year to track how she's doing, it is particularly important to do the exercise when there has been a major change in her financial situation. That might mean when she becomes eligible to receive an employee benefit like a pension, decides it's time to sell the family home, or when Aunt Sally dies and leaves her sister an inheritance. Here is a quick review of how to compute net worth.

Assets. There are five classes of assets. What distinguishes one kind from another is how quickly you can turn it into cash or, put another way, how liquid it is. The more liquid an asset, the easier it is to put a value on it. For instance, you know exactly what the $102.55 in your mother's checking account is worth, but you would probably have to ask a local real estate agent or appraiser to give you an estimate of current worth of her house or condo.

Because of the different levels of liquidity of different assets, we suggest that you separate your assets into these five classes:

Current assets. Current assets are easily convertible into cash. This includes bank accounts, money-market mutual funds, and Treasury securities.

For each of your parent's bank accounts, list the name of the bank where the asset is held, the current balance, and the current yield. Also list the yield on Treasury bills, which mature in a year or less, and U.S. savings bonds, which you can cash in any time as long as you have held them for at least six months. If mom has overpaid her taxes and is due a refund from the Internal Revenue Service (IRS) or your state tax department, you should also count that as a current asset.

Securities. These include publicly traded stocks, bonds, mutual funds, futures contracts, warrants, and options. The current market values of most of these securities are available in most major newspapers, particularly *The Wall Street Journal,* from the most recent brokerage fund statement, and your or mom's broker.

Real estate. Real estate includes first and second homes, condominiums, cooperatives, rental properties, and real estate limited partnerships. If your parent or you are contemplating selling the property, the current worth of all real estate should be based on appraisals from knowledgeable local experts like appraisers or real estate agents. Remember to subtract all selling costs, such as the standard 6 percent real estate broker's commission. For partnerships, list the general managing partner who is running the operation, the yield being paid to you, if any, and the year you expect the partnership to be liquidated and the proceeds to be paid out to you. Also include any mortgage loans that may be due you, such as on a house you sold on which you granted a loan.

Long-term assets. These include the cash value of life insurance policies; the worth of annuities, pensions, and profit-sharing plans; IRAs and Keogh plans; any long-term loans due your mom; any long-term royalties due you from writing a book or having patented an invention that is still selling; and any interests mom may have in an ongoing business.

Long-term assets are often difficult to value. However, mom's life insurance company will give her the current value of policies and annuities, and, if she is still working, her employer will tell her what her pension and profit-sharing plans would be worth if she left the company now.

Valuing her interest in a closely held business is particularly tricky, but it can be done. For example, you could ask her partners what they would be willing to pay if she wanted to cash in her share. (They need to get a formal buy/sell agreement in place if they don't already have one. That agreement will tell you how value is determined. To some extent, that depends on how actively involved in the business she is and how key it is for the business to have her services available.) You may also get some idea from a business broker who specializes in selling and buying the kind of business in which you are involved, or by consulting with a CPA specializing in business valuations.

Personal property. Personal property such as cars, jewelry, collectibles, and home furnishings would be valued at whatever you think they could be sold for now in their present condition. In valuing personal property, try to be as realistic as possible. Don't just put down what you think they are worth; this number is often inflated. You should try to get some sense of the market when you value things. For instance, check with a used-car dealer, the used-car ads in your newspaper, or the National Automobile Dealers Association Blue Book to see what your car's model and year is now worth. Bring any rare coins or stamps into a reputable dealer for an appraisal. For antiques or other collectibles, contact a local member of the American Society of Appraisers. Ask respected antiques investors and dealers for recommendations.

Roadmap 2.1 is an assets worksheet. Use it to make a detailed list not only of mom's assets, but also who holds the titles to them. Some assets, like a securities portfolio for a grandchild, may be held in a trust for which she or the parents are responsible until the child turns 18. If you need more space for any category as you fill out the worksheets, copy that page and attach it to your worksheet.

Liabilities. Liabilities, or what mom owes others, are not as much fun to add up as assets, but you've got to add them up anyway. Just as with the assets, liabilities should be divided into short- and long-term categories, although the older you get the fewer long-term debts, like mortgages, your parent probably has. In Roadmap 2.2 Liabilities Worksheet, list those to whom your mom owes money, the interest rate she is paying, when the loan comes due if there is such a maturity date, and how much money she owes. In general, you should use the following four main categories for listing your liabilities:

Current liabilities. These are debts mom must pay within the next six months. In this category would be bills from the utilities (telephone, electric, gas, oil companies), physicians and dentists, home repair contractors, retail stores, and other short-term creditors. If mom owes money to a relative or friend who helped her out in a pinch, make sure to also include that debt in this category.

Unpaid taxes. These taxes might be due either on April 15 or as part of her quarterly estimated tax payments to both the IRS and her state tax

Roadmap 2.1

Assets Worksheet

Assets	Date Purchased	Purchase Price	Current $ Value
1. Current Assets			
Bonuses or Commissions (due you)	_____	$_____	$_____
Certificates of Deposit	_____	_____	_____
	_____	_____	_____
Checking Accounts	_____	_____	_____
	_____	_____	_____
Credit Union Accounts	_____	_____	_____
Money-Market Accounts	_____	_____	_____
	_____	_____	_____
Savings Accounts	_____	_____	_____
	_____	_____	_____
Savings Bonds	_____	_____	_____
	_____	_____	_____
Tax Refunds (due you)	_____	_____	_____
Treasury Bills	_____	_____	_____
	_____	_____	_____
Total Current Assets		$_____	$_____
2. Securities			
Bonds (type of bond)			
_____	_____	$_____	$_____
_____	_____	_____	_____
_____	_____	_____	_____
_____	_____	_____	_____
Bond Mutual Funds			
_____	_____	_____	_____
_____	_____	_____	_____
Individual Stocks			
_____	_____	_____	_____
_____	_____	_____	_____
_____	_____	_____	_____
_____	_____	_____	_____
_____	_____	_____	_____
_____	_____	_____	_____
Stock Mutual Funds			
_____	_____	_____	_____
_____	_____	_____	_____
_____	_____	_____	_____
_____	_____	_____	_____
Futures	_____	_____	_____
Warrants and Options	_____	_____	_____
Total Securities		$_____	$_____

3. Real Estate

Mortgage Receivable (due you)	$ ____	$ ____
Primary Residence	____	____
Rental Property	____	____
Real Estate Limited Partnerships	____	____
Second Home	____	____
Total Real Estate	$ ____	$ ____

4. Long-Term Assets

Annuities	$ ____	$ ____
IRAs	____	____
Keogh Accounts	____	____
Life Insurance Cash Values	____	____
Loans Receivable (due you)	____	____
Pensions	____	____
Private Business Interests	____	____
Profit-Sharing Plans	____	____
Royalties	____	____
Salary Reduction Plans (401(k), 403(b), 457 plans)	____	____
Total Long-term Assets	$ ____	$ ____

5. Personal Property

Antiques	$ ____	$ ____
Appliances (washing machines, dishwashers, vacuum cleaners, etc.)	____	____
Automobiles	____	____
Boats, etc.	____	____
Campers, Trailers, etc.	____	____
Clothing	____	____
Coin Collections	____	____
Computers, etc.	____	____
Furniture	____	____
Furs	____	____
Home Entertainment Equipment (CD players, stereos, televisions, VCRs, etc.)	____	____
Home Furnishings (drapes, blankets, etc.)	____	____
Jewelry	____	____
Lighting Fixtures	____	____
Motorcycles, etc.	____	____

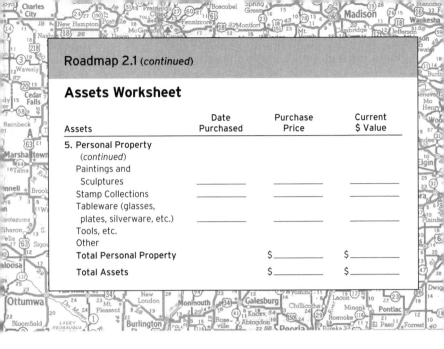

Roadmap 2.1 (continued)

Assets Worksheet

Assets	Date Purchased	Purchase Price	Current $ Value
5. Personal Property (continued)			
Paintings and Sculptures	_____	_____	_____
Stamp Collections	_____	_____	_____
Tableware (glasses, plates, silverware, etc.)	_____	_____	_____
Tools, etc.			
Other			
Total Personal Property		$ _____	$ _____
Total Assets		$ _____	$ _____

department. They include not only income taxes but also the capital gains taxes she might owe on an asset she sold for a profit. You should also include local property taxes, which mom probably pays directly, but which may be paid by the bank that holds her mortgage. If she owes any sales taxes on purchases you have made recently, put that down as well. Finally, if mom is self-employed, make sure to account for Social Security self-employment taxes.

Real estate debt. This category of debt includes both first and second mortgages on mom's primary residence and on any second (or even third) home she may have. It also includes any mortgages she owes on rental properties that are producing income. On a separate line, list any home equity loans outstanding on your first or second home.

Installment debt. Installment debt covers all loans she has committed to pay off over a period of time. This category includes bank loans taken out to consolidate bills or for any other purpose including overdraft loans attached to her checking account; loans to pay for equipment or appliances, such as the refrigerator; home improvement loans; life insurance loans taken against the cash value in her policies; and margin loans from a brokerage house taken against the value of her securities. If she has lost a lawsuit and there is a liability judgment against her, that should be considered part of the installment debt she owes.

Roadmap 2.2

Liabilities Worksheet

Liabilities	To Whom	Interest Rate %	Due Date	Total Balance Due $
1. Current Liabilities				
Alimony	_____	_____ %	_____	$ _____
Bills				
Electric & Gas	_____	_____	_____	_____
Home Contractor	_____	_____	_____	_____
Oil Company	_____	_____	_____	_____
Physician & Dentist	_____	_____	_____	_____
Retail Stores	_____	_____	_____	_____
Telephone	_____	_____	_____	_____
Other	_____	_____	_____	_____
Child Support	_____	_____	_____	_____
Loans to Individuals	_____	_____	_____	_____
Total Current Liabilities				$ _____
2. Unpaid Taxes				
Income Taxes				
Federal	_____	_____ %	_____	$ _____
State	_____	_____	_____	_____
City	_____	_____	_____	_____
Capital Gains Taxes				
Federal	_____	_____	_____	_____
State	_____	_____	_____	_____
City	_____	_____	_____	_____
Property Taxes	_____	_____	_____	_____
Sales Taxes Locality	_____			
Social Security Taxes (self-employed)	_____	_____	_____	_____
Total Unpaid Taxes				$ _____
3. Real Estate Liabilities				
Home #1				
First Mortgage	_____	_____ %	_____	$ _____
Second Mortgage	_____	_____	_____	_____
Home Equity Loan	_____	_____	_____	_____
Home #2				
First Mortgage	_____	_____	_____	_____
Second Mortgage	_____	_____	_____	_____
Home Equity Loan	_____	_____	_____	_____
Rental Property				
First Mortgage	_____	_____	_____	_____
Second Mortgage	_____	_____	_____	_____
Total Real Estate Liabilities				$ _____

Roadmap 2.2 (continued)

Liabilities Worksheet

Liabilities	To Whom	Interest Rate %	Due Date	Total Balance Due $
4. Installment Liabilities				
Automobile Loans	_____	_____%	_____	$ _____
Bill Consolidation Loans	_____	_____	_____	_____
Credit Cards	_____	_____	_____	_____
Education Loans	_____	_____	_____	_____
Equipment and Appliance Loans	_____	_____	_____	_____
Furniture Loans	_____	_____	_____	_____
Home Improvement Loans	_____	_____	_____	_____
Liability Judgments	_____	_____	_____	_____
Life Insurance Loans	_____	_____	_____	_____
Margin Loans Against Securities	_____	_____	_____	_____
Overdraft Bank Loans	_____	_____	_____	_____
Retirement Plan Loans	_____	_____	_____	_____
Total Installment Liabilities				$ _____
Total Liabilities				$ _____

Credit card charges from MasterCard, Visa, American Express, Diners Club, Discover, as well as retail stores, on which you owe at least the minimum payment, should also be noted in this category because you control when to pay off the outstanding balance.

Now, for the moment of truth: Take your total assets from the Roadmap 2.1 and subtract your total liabilities from Roadmap 2.2. This determines your net worth.

Total Assets	$ _____
(Minus) Total Liabilities	(_____)
Equals Positive (or Negative) Net Worth	$ _____

If mom's net worth is positive, assets and liabilities are—at minimum —under control. If her net worth is negative, do not despair. Knowing that her finances are under water (financially speaking) is the first step toward improving her situation.

Smart Money Strategies for Senior Travelers

As your parents get older, certain financial events inevitably are bound to occur, and the more they are prepared for them, the easier it would be to handle them. The relatively small amount of time you and dad spend on planning will pay off enormously for the rest of his life, both in terms of dollars and cents and in the security it gives both of you to know he will be able to deal with almost any twist or turn of his financial fate.

You've now worked together to determine his assets and liabilities; the next step is to determine the cash flow; that's the money coming in from all sources and the money going out for any reason whatsoever. Roadmap 2.3 will guide you through these calculations.

Projecting Expenses and Income. The first step in assembling a realistic long-term plan is to calculate how much money dad will likely need in retirement (we are assuming that dad is no longer working) and to pinpoint his potential sources of income. To some extent, how much money he needs depends on his lifestyle. (Some expenses, such as business clothing, Social Security taxes, life insurance premiums, and job-related costs, should certainly decrease. However, he might be spending more for other expenses, such as hobbies, leisure travel, health care, health insurance, and possibly long-term care insurance.) In addition, inflation will continue to increase your costs over time.

For a rough idea of dad's expenses as the years progress, use the simple worksheet in Roadmap 2.4, which factors in a long-term inflation rate of 4.5 percent. The savings called for in Item 2 include all regular savings. The worksheet's sample figures assume an annual income of $50,000, an annual savings of $5,000, and 20 years until retirement. (Refer to Roadmap 1.1 to determine your dad's projected lifespan.) Use the figures in Roadmap 2.3, Cash Flow Worksheet, to complete this worksheet.

With this general idea of how much money dad will need each year, examine his potential sources of income. The three main income sources for retirees are Social Security, pensions, and private savings and investments. Ask yourselves these questions: Does he currently have enough in savings

Roadmap 2.3

Cash Flow Worksheet

Annual Income	$ Amount	$ Total
1. Earned Income		
Salary after Deductions	$_____	
Bonuses	_____	
Commissions	_____	
Deferred Compensation	_____	
Overtime	_____	
Stock Options	_____	
Tips	_____	
Other	_____	
Total Earned Income		$_____
2. Self-Employment Income		
Freelance Income	$_____	
Income from Partnerships	_____	
Income from Running a Small Business	_____	
Rental Income from Real Estate	_____	
Royalties	_____	
Other	_____	
Total Self-employment Income		$_____
3. Family Income		
Alimony Income	$_____	
Child Support Income	_____	
Family Trust Income	_____	
Gifts from Family Members	_____	
Inheritance Income	_____	
Other	_____	
Total Family Income		$_____
4. Government Income		
Aid to Families with Dependent Children Income	$_____	
Disability Insurance Income	_____	
Unemployment Insurance Income	_____	
Veterans Benefits	_____	
Welfare Income	_____	
Workers' Compensation Income	_____	

Other _____

Total Government Income $ _____

5. Retirement Income

Annuity Payments $ _____

Social Security Income _____

Pension Income _____

Income from IRAs _____

Income from Keogh Accounts _____

Income from Profit-Sharing Accounts _____

Income from Salary Reduction Plans
(401(k), 403(b), 457 plans) _____

Other _____

Total Retirement Income $ _____

6. Investment Income

Bank Account Interest

CDs $ _____

Money-Market Accounts _____

NOW Accounts _____

Saving Accounts _____

Bonds and Bond Funds

Capital Gains _____

Dividends _____

Interest _____

Other _____

Limited Partnerships (real estate,
oil, gas) _____

Money Funds and T-Bills

Taxable Funds _____

Tax-Exempt Funds _____

T-Bills _____

Stock and Stock Funds

Capital Gains _____

Dividends _____

Interest _____

Other _____

Other _____

Total Investment Income $ _____

7. Other Income (specify)

_____ $ _____

Total Other Income $ _____

Total Annual Income $ _____

Annual Expenses	$ Amount	$ Total
1. Fixed Expenses		
Automobile-Related	$ _____	
Car Payment (loan or lease)	_____	
Gasoline or Oil	_____	
Other	_____	
Total		$ _____
Family		
Alimony	_____	
Child Support Payments	_____	
Food and Beverage	_____	
School Tuition	_____	
Other	_____	
Total		$ _____
Home-Related		
Mortgage Payments #1	_____	
Mortgage Payments #2	_____	
Rent	_____	
Total		$ _____
Insurance		
Auto	_____	
Disability	_____	
Dental	_____	
Health	_____	
Homeowners	_____	
Life	_____	
Other	_____	
Total		$ _____
Savings, Investments, and Loans		
Bank Loan Repayment	_____	
Emergency Fund Contributions	_____	
Salary Reduction Plans	_____	
Contributions (401(k), 403(b), 457 plans)	_____	
Other	_____	
Total		$ _____
Taxes		
Federal	_____	
Local	_____	
Property	_____	
Social Security (self-employed)	_____	
State	_____	

Other	_____	
Total		$_____
Utilities		
Electricity	_____	
Gas	_____	
Telephone	_____	
Water and Sewage	_____	
Cable Television	_____	
Other	_____	
Total		$_____
Other (specify)		
_____	_____	
Total		$_____
Total Fixed Expenses		$_____

2. Flexible Expenses

Children		
Allowances	$_____	
Babysitting	_____	
Books	_____	
Camp Fees	_____	
Day Care	_____	
Events (parties, class trips, etc.)	_____	
Toys	_____	
Other	_____	
Total		$_____
Clothing		
New Purchases	_____	
Shoes	_____	
Upkeep (cleaning, tailoring, dry cleaning, etc.)	_____	
Total		$_____
Contributions and Dues		
Charitable Donations	_____	
Gifts (Christmas, birthdays, etc.)	_____	
Political Contributions	_____	
Religious Contributions	_____	
Union Dues	_____	
Other	_____	
Total		$_____
Education		
Room and Board	_____	

Annual Expenses	$ Amount	$ Total
Books and Supplies (parents and/or children)	_____	
Tuition (parents and/or children)	_____	
Other	_____	
Total		$_____
Equipment and Vehicles		
Appliance Purchases and Maintenance	_____	
Car, Boat, and Other Vehicle Purchases and Maintenance	_____	
Computer Purchases, etc.	_____	
Consumer Electronics Purchases	_____	
Licenses and Registration of Cars, Boats, etc.	_____	
Parking	_____	
Other	_____	
Total		$_____
Financial and Professional Services		
Banking Fees	_____	
Brokerage Commissions and Fees	_____	
Financial Advice	_____	
Legal Advice	_____	
Tax Preparation Fees	_____	
Other	_____	
Total		$_____
Food		
Alcohol	_____	
Foods and Snacks at Home	_____	
Restaurant Meals and Snacks	_____	
Tobacco	_____	
Other	_____	
Total		$_____
Home Maintenance		
Garbage Removal	_____	
Garden Supplies and Maintenance	_____	
Home Office Supplies	_____	
Home Furnishings	_____	
Home or Apartment Repairs and Renovations	_____	
Home Cleaning Services	_____	
Home Supplies	_____	
Lawn Care and Snow Removal	_____	

Linens	_____
Uninsured Casualty or Theft Loss	_____
Other	_____
Total	$_____

Medical Care

Dental Care	_____
Drugs (over the counter)	_____
Drugs (prescriptions)	_____
Eye care and Eyeglasses	_____
Hospital (uninsured portion)	_____
Medical Devices (wheelchairs, canes, etc.)	_____
Medical Expenses (parents, etc.)	_____
Nursing Home Fees (parents, etc.)	_____
Personal Beauty Care (hair stylist, manicurist, etc.)	_____
Personal Care (cosmetics, toiletries, etc.)	_____
Physician Bills	_____
Unreimbursed Medical Expenses	_____
Other	_____
Total	$_____

Miscellaneous

Mystery Cash	_____
Postage and Stamps	_____
Recurring Nonrecurring Expenses	_____
Unreimbursed Business Expenses	_____
Other	_____
Total	$_____

Recreation and Entertainment

Animal Care	_____
Books	_____
Club Dues	_____
Cultural Events	_____
Health Club Memberships	_____
Hobbies	_____
Lottery Tickets	_____
Magazine and Newspaper Subscriptions	_____
Movie Admissions	_____
Music Admissions	_____
Photography (cameras, developing, film, etc.)	_____
Play Admissions	_____

Annual Expenses	$ Amount	$ Total
Recreational Equipment (games, sports, etc.)	_____	
Sporting Events Admission	_____	
Videotape Rentals	_____	
Other	_____	
Total		$_____
Savings and Investments		
Bank Savings Contributions	_____	
Stock, Bond, and Mutual Fund Contributions	_____	
IRA Contributions	_____	
Keogh Account Contributions	_____	
401(k)/403(b)	_____	
Other	_____	
Total		$_____
Travel and Vacations		
Bus Fares	_____	
Subway Costs	_____	
Tolls	_____	
Train Fares	_____	
Travel Expenses (other than vacations)	_____	
Unreimbursed Business Travel Expenses	_____	
Vacations (airfare)	_____	
Vacations (car rental)	_____	
Vacations (food)	_____	
Vacations (hotel)	_____	
Vacations (other)	_____	
Other	_____	
Total		$_____
Other (specify)		
_____	_____	
Total		$_____
Total Flexible Expenses		$_____
Total Annual Expenses (Fixed + Flexible)		$_____
Total Annual Income		$_____
(Minus)		
Total Annual Expenses		(_____)
(Equals)		
Total Net Annual Positive (Or Negative) Cash Flow		$_____

Roadmap 2.4

Retirement Expenses Worksheet

	Example	Your Situation
1. Present Gross Annual Income	$50,000	$_____
2. Present Annual Savings	$ 5,000	$_____
3. Current Spending (Subtract item 2 from item 1.)	$45,000	$_____
4. Retirement Spending Level (between 80 percent and 90 percent, depending on your lifestyle)	90%	_____%
5. Annual Cost of Living (in Today's Dollars) if You Retire Now (Multiply item 4 by item 3.)	$40,500	$_____
6. 4.5 Percent Inflation Factor (from table below)	2.4	_____
7. Estimated Annual Cost of Living (in Future Dollars) at Retirement (Multiply item 6 by item 5.)	$97,200	$_____

Years until Retirement	Inflation Factor
20	2.4
15	1.9
10	1.6
5	1.2

and investments and other sources of income? If yes, how should he draw down his portfolio to ensure that his nest egg lasts as long as he does? Last, you must determine how much he can afford to withdraw and which types of accounts he should take the money from first.

As with most things financial, the answer is that the appropriate amount to withdraw each year depends on dad's circumstances and goals. The safe withdrawal rate is approximately 4 to 5 percent of the total account balance per year, according to several studies.

While the studies limited the investment mix to two asset classes (an S&P 500 index fund and short-term fixed income securities), they showed that longer payout periods (30 to 40 years) necessitate that portfolios have concentrations in equities.

For example, if you had a $1 million portfolio, you could safely withdraw approximately 4.5 percent, or $45,000, the first year in retirement. The $45,000 withdrawal would supplement any Social Security and pension benefits you may have. Assuming a 3 percent inflation rate and the same asset balance, next year's withdrawal would be $46,350 (1.03 × $45,000), and so on. Under such circumstances, and assuming your father is 65 and in good health, limiting his retirement withdrawals to this safe withdrawal rate offers a good chance of realizing portfolio growth to support his needs throughout retirement. Tollbooth 2.1 gives a bird's-eye-view of how long $100,000 would last at different rates of return and different withdrawal amounts, and assumes you are willing to deplete your accumulated savings. It is offered only as an example of how long your money would last under various scenarios.

If dad does not have the assets required to support his lifestyle and meet the safe withdrawal rate, here are some options he might consider.

1. If he has not yet retired, continue working full-time (if health permits),
2. Reduce his living expenses,
3. Work part time after he retires.

Generally, retirement assets will last longer if you draw on taxable assets first. Therefore, refrain from drawing down the tax-deferred assets like 401(k)s, 403(b)s, and IRAs for as long as possible. This allows the tax-deferred assets to continue to receive tax deferral for a longer period of time. The higher the tax bracket, the more important it is to draw first on taxable assets.

For the taxable category, first draw down assets with a loss or the least amount of capital gain, so that you can lock in capital losses for tax benefits

Tollbooth 2.1

How Many Years Will $100,000 Last?

Yearly Withdrawals	Required Annual Rate of Return				
	4%	5%	6%	8%	10%
$ 5,000	20	22	25	26	Should be perpetual
7,500	13	14	15	18	24
10,000	10	10	11	12	14
12,500	8	8	8.5	9	10
15,000	6.5	6.5	7	7.5	8

*Assumes a single withdrawal at the start of every year beginning the first year and increasing that amount by 4 percent in subsequent years to account for inflation.

and/or reduce the amount of capital gains taxes. Selling investments by matching capital losses and gains can also minimize the total tax impact.

If your dad never paid taxes on the contributions that he put put into his retirement accounts, all distributions will be fully taxable as ordinary income. The order of distributing specific assets within retirement accounts is generally immaterial from a tax standpoint. Tax-deferred assets acquired partially with after-tax dollars (nondeductible IRA) should be distributed before the fully taxable retirement assets to defer more income tax liability into later years. All of his retirement assets should usually be distributed before tapping into a Roth IRA.

Hazard!
Tax Trap

If dad expects to leave assets to his children or other heirs, and if he has unusually large capital gains on certain stocks or mutual funds held outside of retirement accounts, it may make sense to hold the securities and pass these on to the heirs. When dad dies, the investment's cost basis is stepped up to its current market value before being transferred to his heirs, erasing the capital gains and the built-up tax liability.

Gone Fishin': How to Create a Stream of Income After Retirement

Now that you know how much dad can safely withdraw from his portfolio, how should he set up his investments to get some money out? The easiest way is to transfer the money he needs to live on via a monthly direct deposit from a money market fund. Therefore, do the following:

1. Set up a money market fund within each brokerage account he may own. Instead of reinvesting interest, dividends, and capital gains received on his mutual funds or stocks, channel those funds into a money market account that has free check-writing priviledges. Then the money can be transferred to your household checking account as needed.

2. Monitor the money market fund to be sure it always has enough cash for at least three months of living expenses. Because you will be taxed on the distribution discussed in step 1, a portion of these distributions must be set aside to pay the taxes.

3. If his assets continue to grow, and he foresees not outliving the money, he might want to take advantage of the estate planning laws to gift money free of estate tax. (It's more beneficial to gift appreciated stock or stock funds instead of cash to avoid future capital gains taxes.)

   If the interest, dividends, and/or capital gains are not enough to meet living expenses, dad will periodically need to sell some investments. While some general guidelines for the sale of assets apply, he really needs to look at the overall picture to figure out what works best for him. Strategies might include the following:

   ▶ Selling assets to maintain his overall asset allocation. For example, if bonds represent a higher percentage of his assets than he would prefer, reduce his exposure to bonds. If his equity investments have appreciated significantly compared to his fixed-income investments, rebalance the portfolio back to his target allocation by selling some equities. Most advisors suggest rebalancing at least annually.

   ▶ Selling assets that create the least taxable gain. Examples: Lock in stock losses, offset gains with losses, or sell bonds, which generally have minimal capital gains.

4. Use tax-deferred retirement accounts (401(k), 403(b), IRA, etc.) for retirement cash flow only after taxable accounts are spent down, un-

less withdrawals are needed to meet required minimum distributions (RMD). If dad is over 70½ set aside his annual RMD in a money market fund within his retirement account. Direct all distributions of interest, dividends, and/or capital gains to be paid out as cash distributions to help replenish his money market fund. Then money from this money market fund can be transferred into his checking account on a monthly or yearly basis.

If the interest, dividends, and/or capital gains are not enough to meet living expenses, he will need to sell assets while maintaining his overall asset allocation.

If dad is under age 59½ and forced to withdraw money from his retirement plans, don't forget to factor in the 10 percent early withdrawal penalty as well as income tax payments when determining the amount of money he can spend on living expenses.

5. As indicated earlier, use tax-advantaged accounts only after taxable accounts are spent down. Postpone tapping into his Roth IRA assets (if he has them) as long as possible. Generally, Roth accounts should be the last assets you access. Be sure to maintain your overall asset allocation on your total portfolio.

Determining how much to withdraw to fund dad's living expenses is the first step. Next, work to simplify the withdrawal process. Remember, utilize the interest, dividends, and capital gains that the investments generate to provide cash to pay taxes, and fund living expenses. Don't forget to include RMD when you're determining how much cash dad will need. General guidelines: Tap taxable accounts, then tax-deferred, then Roth.

Protecting Your Parent's Income from the Customs Inspector

In all likelihood, your parents will pay fewer taxes once they retire because their lack of salary places them in a lower tax bracket, but their combined income from pensions, Social Security, individual retirement accounts (IRAs), Keogh plans, annuities, and investments may keep them in the same tax bracket as before they retired. To minimize the tax bite, your parents should withdraw their retirement income in a way that will postpone their tax liability for as long as possible.

For example, unless they absolutely need the capital to live on, they should not take distributions from their IRAs or Keoghs until they reach age

70½. This strategy allows the maximum amount of time for their assets to accumulate tax deferred. If they withdraw funds from an insurance contract, they should first take out their original principal, which is not taxable, then receive distributions from investment earnings, which are subject to taxation. If they are in the top tax bracket, they may want to sell investments producing taxable income, such as Treasury or corporate bonds, and buy municipal bonds paying tax-free income. If they live in a high-tax state, they should buy bonds issued by that state to sidestep both federal and state taxes.

In addition, they should take full advantage of the many provisions in the tax code aimed at senior citizens. The following provisions apply to anyone 65 and older:

▶ Must file a return only if they report a gross income of $9,150 or more for a single person, or $17,800 for a married couple, both over 65, filing jointly.

▶ If they do not itemize, they qualify for a higher standard deduction of as much as $11,600.

▶ May qualify for a tax credit if they do not receive Social Security or railroad retirement benefits.

▶ Generally, up to 50 percent of their Social Security benefits will be taxable. However, up to 85% of benefits can be taxable if either of the following situations applies: The total of one-half of the benefits and all other income is more than $34,000 ($44,000 if you are married filing jointly).

▶ If they move into a continuing-care or life-care community, the portion of their monthly fees allocated to health care services is deductible as an itemized medical expense.

▶ Mapping the Route: Living on a Fixed Income

Social Security, pensions, IRAs, and the capital your parent accumulated through regular savings and investment programs are the most common sources of retirement income. Depending on how much your parents receive from Social Security, company-sponsored pension plans, and their own tax-sheltered IRA, Keogh, or SEP, their private savings may amount to anywhere from 30 to 50 percent of their retirement income. If they are not eligible for pensions and have not funded their own tax-sheltered plan, their private savings are all that separates them from living on Social Security—potentially a meager existence. In this section, we will briefly look at each of these as a refresher to give you a handle on what to expect and how best to optimize their usefulness to your mom or dad.

Social Security. An important aspect of your mom's income calculation is the amount that she will receive from Social Security. Don't believe the prophecies that the Social Security system will go broke within just the next few years. If you are reading this book, it is likely that your parent is already receiving Social Security, in which case, she may receive smaller increases or, depending on other income, may have to pay higher taxes on her Social Security income, but you can anticipate that Social Security will be part of her income mix.

If you are planning for the future, here are a few ways that Social Security may be altered (depending on your parent's age, even these changes may not affect her benefits):

1. A means test may allocate a smaller benefit to higher income people.
2. A person will be penalized for retiring earlier than the full retirement age (FRA). Even under today's law, you receive only 80 percent of your full Social Security benefit if you retire at age 62. Under current rules, this percentage will drop annually until it reaches 70 percent by the year 2022. It is possible that the percentage will drop even more than that as Congress seeks ways to trim Social Security spending.
3. The minimum age for receiving full Social Security benefits will rise gradually from age 65 to 67. Currently, this affects people born in 1938 and later. For example, if dad was born in 1940, his minimum retirement age will be 65½. If mom was born in 1950, her minimum retirement age will be 66. For those born in 1960 or later, their FRA will be 67. In the future, the minimum age will probably be extended even further.
4. People will be encouraged to retire later. Under current law, Social Security benefits grow 5 percent a year for every year you delay retirement, up to age 70. This rate will increase in the future until it reaches 8 percent per year for people turning 65 in 2008 or later. This incentive might be sweetened even more over time.
5. Taxes on Social Security benefits may increase. You must pay tax on as much as 85 percent of your benefits if your provisional income, which includes tax-exempt municipal bond interest, plus one half of your Social Security benefit exceeds $44,000 for married couples filing jointly or $34,000 for all other filers except married couples filing separately. Those

married filing separately are also subject to the 85 percent threshold when provisional income is greater than $34,000.

6. The percentage of your pre-retirement pay that Social Security is designed to replace will likely be reduced from the current 24 percent to 20 percent or less.

7. Social Security payroll taxes will increase from the current 7.65 percent for employees and employers.

All of these changes mean that Social Security will likely make up an increasingly smaller percentage of a person's retirement income in the years ahead, so if you are reading this to prepare for the future, keep this fact in mind.

How Early Retirement Affects Social Security Benefits. If mom is 62, should she take Social Security now or wait until her full retirement age? The first issue you and she should consider is whether she needs the payments for cash-flow purposes. If she does, start the payments as soon as possible. If she doesn't need them, a number of factors need to be considered, including inflation, risk, opportunity cost, earnings limitations, and tax impact.

If mom starts drawing benefits at age 62, they always will be less than the FRA benefits, although total *expected* benefits during her "expected" lifetime will be approximately the same either way. (You either receive more payments of a smaller benefit or fewer payments of a larger benefit.)

Early benefits are 20 percent to 30 percent less than the FRA depending on the number of months to FRA. With the benefit statement Social Security sends each year in hand, you and mom can work through the items below to make a decision.

1. Inflation. Any dollar received today is worth more than tomorrow's due to inflation, which continually erodes purchasing power. Social Security, however, takes into account inflation with a Cost-of-Living Allowance (COLA) that applies to everyone at age 62, whether they take benefits or not. Whenever you decide to take your benefits after age 62, the annual COLA adjusts the amount—it was 2.7 percent in 2005.

2. Risk. The longer a person puts off drawing benefits, the greater the risk of dying before the total from larger, later payments catches up with that of the smaller, earlier payments you could have elected. To calculate your mother's crossover point, take her projected monthly benefit at both age 62 and at FRA, add the monthly cumulative total during

her life expectancy (about age 84 to 86), then find the month when the cumulative FRA benefit either equals or exceeds the early retirement benefit. At this crossover point, you will have collected roughly the same amount under either retirement age. Then, carefully consider your family's longevity and her personal well-being to evaluate the likelihood that she will survive beyond the crossover point.

3. Opportunity Cost. Most financial decisions involve opportunity cost, in this case the dollar amount mom could have realized from taking the benefit earlier and investing it. To determine that, assume an appropriate rate of return for an investment that would have to be sold to replace the Social Security income. Then do the numbers from age 62 until the time you expect mom will need the money.

4. Earnings Limitations. Effective in 2005, the Social Security earnings limit is $1,000 per month or $12,000 per year for individuals between age 62 and full retirement age who are receiving benefits. One dollar of every two in Social Security benefits will be withheld for each dollar earned over the limit. In the year you reach your FRA: $1 in benefits will be deducted for each $3 you earn above the limit, but this affects only earnings made *before* the month you reach FRA. For 2005, this limit is $31,800. Exceptions to earned income limits include pensions, retirement pay, dividends, interest, capital gains, and rental income as well as 401(k) and IRA withdrawals.

   It may not make sense to begin Social Security if your benefits will be reduced due to other earnings. The earnings limits are adjusted annually and can be found at http://www.ssa.gov.

5. Tax Impact. Up to 85 percent of Social Security benefits are taxable at your individual income tax rate, which depends on your Modified Adjusted Gross Income (MAGI). If your federal tax rate is 28 percent, you will owe Uncle Sam 28 cents of each $1 of the first 85 percent of your annual Social Security benefits. Also, including Social Security benefits in your AGI may limit the deductions for medical expenses or other itemized deductions that are based on percentages of AGI.

Survivor's Benefits. If dad has recently died, your mother is entitled to widow's benefits (if it was the opposite way around, your father would be entitled to the same benefits). Most funeral directors will notify Social Security of an individual's death, or you or your mother can do it yourselves. She is eligible to receive full benefits at full retirement age (currently age 65) or reduced benefits as early as age 60 or, if she is disabled, she qualifies as early as age 50. Other survivor's benefits are available to young or disabled children as well as to widow(er)s caring for young children. For more information, visit the Social Security Web site, http://www.ssa.gov, stop by your local Social Security office, or call the Social Security Administration at 800-772-1213.

Supplemental Security Income. For those with extremely low incomes and few assets, an additional source of retirement funds is Supplemental Security Income (SSI). The SSI program is run by the Social Security Administration, though benefits are paid from the U.S. Treasury, not the Social Security Trust Fund. To qualify for SSI, you must be a U.S. citizen living in the United States, and you must be 65 or older, blind, or disabled. The maximum income you can receive from private or government pensions or earn from a job differs by state. However, the government sets a national limit of $2,000 worth of assets for one person and $3,000 for a couple to qualify for SSI. When totaling assets, the Social Security Administration does not include the value of your home, your car, or many of your personal belongings. Instead, it focuses on assets in bank and brokerage accounts and cash.

If you qualify for SSI, your benefit depends on how much you earn and where you live. However, as of 2005 the basic national benefit, which changes over time, is $579 a month for an individual and $869 for a couple. Many states augment this basic benefit. SSI is also available to non-retired people with disabilities. To learn more about rules for qualification, and benefit levels in your state, contact a local Social Security office, or call the Social Security Administration (Telephone: 800-772-1213; http://www.ssa.gov).

Pension Benefits. No matter how much Social Security your father qualifies for, as a sole source of income, it is clearly not enough to maintain a comfortable standard of living. If you are reading this book, it is probably too late to begin any sort of plan for your parent, but if he is qualified to receive benefits, it's important for you to understand their ramifications.

There are two forms of pensions: one your employer provides without any contribution from you, and one to which you contribute part of your earnings during your working years, either through your employer or through a separate plan, such as an IRA or a Keogh account. In the best of all worlds, your parents will qualify for both types of pensions.

Defined Benefit Plans. If your parent(s) qualify, defined benefit plans can provide a substantial portion—from 10 to 40 percent—of their total retirement income. The amount they receive often depends on how many years your parent worked for the employer and their salary during the final few years at the company. The longer your parent worked for the employer and the higher the salary, the fatter the monthly pension check.

If your parent is entitled to a pension and is not receiving it, contact the company's employee benefits department. Your parent should be receiving a yearly statement from the department detailing all of the entitled benefits, including pension benefits. If dad didn't receive one, request a personalized benefits statement, which will describe his monthly pension benefit.

Defined benefit pension plans guarantee in advance the size of an individual's monthly pension benefit. If the company does not make the needed contributions, if investment returns fall short or, in the most extreme case, if the company goes out of business, pension payments are made from the remaining pension fund and, if necessary, from the federally backed Pension Benefit Guaranty Corporation (PBGC). (However, the PBGC does impose a maximum annual pension benefit, which in 2005 was $45,613.68 for a person retiring at age 65; this amount increases with inflation every year.)

While dad might be assured of receiving pension payments, he is by no means guaranteed that those payments, combined with Social Security, will adequately fund his retirement. Most pension benefits are fixed at the time you retire, so inflation slowly erodes the value of the benefits. (A few generous pension plans provide a cost-of-living adjustment for benefits, but don't count on it.) In addition, companies looking for ways to cut expenses can institute payment formulas that will reduce your benefit upon retirement. In the most extreme cases, companies will terminate their pension plans altogether before you begin receiving benefits and substitute an annuity purchased from an insurance company that will provide a fixed benefit, usually less than you would have earned from the pension plan directly. Such a substitution also replaces the ultimate backing of your pension payment from the federal PBGC with that of the insurance company. (Annuities are discussed in greater detail later in this section.)

As long as your dad was vested, mom will receive pension benefits, even if the he dies before retirement. If this is your parent's situation, and she is not collecting benefits, contact the company's benefits department to find out about survivor's coverage. Usually the spousal benefit begins starting in the year the employee would have stopped working, usually age 65. This is known as a pre-retirement survivor's annuity. Most pension plans will also

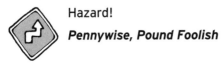

Hazard!
Pennywise, Pound Foolish

Let's suppose dad worked for a company with a defined benefit plan. If your mom signed a document waiving the right to the pre-retirement survivor's annuity, when your dad retired, they would earn a larger pension benefit. However, if dad dies before retirement, mom will not receive a pension from the company.

Unfortunately, if mom is in this position, you can't do a thing about it now; if dad is alive and working, make certain both parents understand this important rule.

continue payments to the spouse for some percentage of the benefit once the primary employee dies if they opt for a joint and survivor payout.

If your parent has changed jobs over the course of a lifetime, the pension benefits from the former employer are locked at the level earned when the employee left the company. They may have been offered the option of receiving the pension benefit in a lump sum, but if not don't forget to apply to the former employer for any pension benefits to which mom or dad might be entitled.

Defined Contribution Plans. If your parent's employer does not offer a traditional defined benefit pension plan, it probably offers a defined contribution plan, which gave the employee the opportunity to put aside money from their salary on a tax-deferred basis until they retire. The employer may or may not match some or all of the contribution. To qualify for participation in a company's plan, a person usually must work there for at least one year. Any money that your parent contributed to a defined contribution plan is always vested, meaning that you can take it with you or roll it over into another firm's plan or an IRA when terminating employment. If you are not sure what decisions your parents made regarding these plans, check with each company's benefits department. There may be hidden cash in those vaults.

Veteran's Benefits. If your parent was an armed forces veteran, he might qualify for an additional pension benefit. You may also be eligible to receive reimbursement of burial and funeral expenses from both federal and state veterans programs, as long as you file a claim within two years of your parent's death.

Salary Reduction Plans. The most common type of defined contribution plan is a salary reduction plan, known as 401(k), 403(b), or 457 plans; federal employees can sign up for the federal thrift savings fund. Though there are differences, they work basically the same way. Your employer deducts a percentage of your salary—usually between 2 and 25 percent, according to your wishes—and deposits the funds in your plan account. The money is deducted from your salary before being taxed at the federal, state, or local level. They are, however, subject to Social Security taxes on the whole amount. As a result, the earnings you report to the IRS are lessened by the amount of your annual contribution. The money you set aside, whether or not it is matched by your employer, is invested in a range of stock, bond, and money market options, and all investment earnings accumulate tax deferred. You pay taxes only when you withdraw the money at retirement.

Again, if you are not certain what, if any, plans your parents have, check with their employers. If your parent has such an account, check the asset allocation.

Pension Plans for the Self-Employed. Keogh and Simplified Employee Pension (SEP) Plans come in several forms. If your parent was self-employed or worked for a small business with one of these plans, they may be entitled to a monthly or lump-sum benefit, so don't overlook this source of income.

Individual Retirement Accounts (IRAs). Even if dad had a defined benefit or defined contribution plan through his employer, or a Keogh or SEP, he may have been funding an IRA as well. In addition, if mom did not have earned income, he might have contributed to a spousal IRA; if she worked outside the home, she may have set up her own IRA. Contributions to IRAs can be made tax deductible under certain circumstances, so when it is time to withdraw money for retirement, it's important to know how the contributions were made as it will affect whether or not taxes will be owed.

> *You can continue to contribute to a traditional IRA until you reach age 70½ presuming you have earned income, at which point you must start withdrawing capital according to an IRS schedule.*

Both spouses may contribute to a Roth IRA if they have earned income, even after they reach age 70½. In addition, they can withdraw all of the principal and earnings totally tax free after age 59½, as long as the assets have remained in the IRA for at least five years after making the first contribution. The assets may also be withdrawn tax free if they are hit by a major disability. In addition, if a person dies before withdrawing the money from a Roth, the proceeds go to the beneficiaries tax free.

Unlike regular IRAs, if your dad can afford it, he does not have to take distributions from a Roth IRA starting at age 70½. In fact, he doesn't have to take distributions at all if he prefers, allowing him to pass the assets in the Roth to his beneficiaries income-tax-free. This is partly because you do not receive a deduction when you contribute to a Roth IRA.

To maximize a traditional IRA tax shelter, dad should keep his money in it as long as possible. He is allowed to withdraw from the account without penalty starting at age 59½, and must begin distributions by age 70½. If he takes out money before age 59½, he will owe a 10 percent early withdrawal penalty, and he must pay income taxes on the distribution in the year he receives it. Unlike salary reduction plans, IRAs do not allow you to borrow against your IRA under any circumstance or withdraw assets without penalty, except under the following conditions:

► The owner of the IRA dies and the proceeds are distributed to a beneficiary or the estate.
► The person becomes permanently disabled.
► The amount distributed is paid out as an annuity over the person's lifetime or life expectancy in substantially equal amounts.

If dad has a traditional IRA and he turns 70½, he has to begin withdrawing at least a minimum amount of money each year thereafter. He must receive the first payment by April 1 of the year after he turns 70½. (Note: His second distribution must be taken by December 31 of that same year he turns 70½.) The IRS requires him to withdraw an equal amount of his account each year based on a uniform actuarial table. If he doesn't take out enough, the IRS will impose a whopping penalty of 50 percent of the difference between what he withdrew and what he should have withdrawn.

The rules also make it easy for your parent to select and change the beneficiary of their IRA account. They can even select a new beneficiary after payouts have begun, and their heirs can even change the beneficiary after they have died. This is so important, because the RMA payout rate is based on the beneficiary's life expectancy. So if the beneficiary is changed to a much younger person, like a grandchild, the payout can take place over many more years and allow the account to grow tax deferred for many more years than if the beneficiary were middle-aged.

Another way to draw on dad's IRA is to take the entire balance in a lump sum.

However, this subjects him to an enormous tax, which leaves less money to reinvest to generate the income on which he must live during retirement. He may also use the proceeds of his IRA to buy an annuity. An annuity makes monthly payments to you for the rest of your life or, if you choose a joint and survivor payout option, for the rest of your life and that of your spouse.

Life insurance. If your mom has funded a cash-value policy—such as whole life, variable life, or universal life—for many years, she probably has built up considerable cash value. Either she can let that cash value continue to accumulate tax deferred, or she can tap that asset by converting it into an annuity (see below) that pays monthly income for the rest of her life or for the rest of both her life and her spouse's life. She may also be able to borrow the cash value out of the policy while keeping the policy in place.

Annuities. One investment designed for retirees is the annuity, which is sold by insurance companies. They can provide a steady stream of income for as long as your parents live. Your parents might find that the best way to convert a large portion of their accumulated savings into a reliable monthly check is to buy an annuity with a good payout plan.

Think of annuities as the opposite of life insurance. Instead of a lump sum payment at death, as with life insurance, an annuity, if your parent annuitizes one, will provide her with a lifelong income stream. Issuers of annuities, insurance companies, invest your contributions. Then, by using actuarially determined life spans, the issuers can forecast the appropriate rate of return for you and the company.

The growth inside an annuity is not taxed at current rates. Instead, it's deferred until paid out to your mother. The payment consists of two parts: the return of her original investment (not taxed) and growth in the account (taxable upon distribution as ordinary income). Once mom's original investment is returned, income from an annuity is completely taxable.

Annuities are categorized as either fixed or variable. Fixed annuities are similar to bonds and certificates of deposit. They guarantee a fixed rate of return for a stated period of time. Some fixed annuities include an option where rates adjust during the accumulation period. However, the rate becomes fixed during distribution. A straight life annuity provides lifelong income with payments ending at the annuity holder's death.

Payments may be guaranteed for certain periods of time (five, 10, or 15 years), with any undistributed portion returned to a beneficiary at the annuity holder's death.

Surrender charges on fixed annuities can be high, but these charges decline annually. All annuities, variable or fixed, are subject to a 10 percent penalty if redeemed before age 59½ with rare exception. It's important to understand that all annuities are relatively non-liquid compared to most commonly held securities.

Variable annuities consist of an annuity contract where mom's payment is based on the performance of various sub-accounts (mutual funds) that were chosen by her. As with fixed annuities, income from a variable annuity does not qualify for long-term capital gains taxation. Variable annuities may provide some death benefits for your parent's estate.

Investing Strategies for a Long Trip

Investments. Getting older doesn't always mean you should be more conservative. Although that statement at first may seem counterintuitive, growing older does not necessarily mean that mom should pull out of stocks altogether. To understand this better, consider the concept of time horizon. Miscalculating or misunderstanding this concept is one of the biggest mistakes an individual can make when it comes to investments.

The time horizon is the amount of time until your parents begin to use some or all of their investments. For example, if you plan to save for a down payment on a new house in two years, your investment time horizon is two years. If you're saving for a child's first year of college and that child is currently 10 years old, your investment time horizon is eight years (when the child is age 18 and ready for school).

There is of course a key difference between investing once you are retired and other investment goals. Most investment goals happen once—car purchases or home purchases, for example. But retirement begins on a certain date and continues over a long period of time. Mom will need the investment proceeds from her retirement planning over a long period.

Based on historical averages, inflation doubles your cost of living every 18 years and has averaged 4 percent per year over the last several decades. Meanwhile, over the long term, the average rate of return for bonds has been about 6 percent and for stocks about 10 percent. The difference between an investment's rate of return and inflation is known as the real rate of return. Mom should want a high real rate of return on her long-term investments without sacrificing too much safety of principal.

Combining the facts that most retirements occur over a long time horizon, inflation continues each year, and stocks have a history of outperforming inflation by the largest margin, you arrive at one conclusion: If feasible, stocks need to be at least some part of most portfolios.

The Five-Year to Seven-Year Timeframe. Historically, it takes stocks five to seven years to complete a full cycle—going from a high, to a low, and back to a new high again. The danger of putting money in stocks for less than a full cycle is that you may catch the down part of the cycle and lose out.

Consider a person, 58, who plans to retire in two years and, therefore, will need to withdraw a small portion of the investments at that time. Meanwhile, the biggest chunk of their money will need to remain invested so that it outpaces inflation. That means stocks. The trick, of course, is to control the percentage you've allocated to stocks and adjust that percentage over time as the time horizons of your mom's life change. You can make some educated guesses as to when mom will need to generate cash from her investments using Roadmap 1.1. Of course, in addition to factoring her income and expenses, you must consider what you know about her health, her family's medical history (Roadmap 1.3), and so on.

As we said, older people are sometimes tempted to convert their investment portfolio from a broad mix of stocks, bonds, and cash instruments to solely income-oriented bonds. That could be the worst investment move they'd ever make. If mom lived for another 30 or 40 years, not only would her portfolio have to provide her with current income, it must also protect her against inflation. Therefore, if she locked herself into current yields by buying only bonds, her capital will not grow as it most likely would if she owned stocks.

As a rule of thumb, by the time a person retires in their 60s, they should have about 40 percent of their money in equities and 60 percent in various fixed-income instruments. Therefore, do not make the mistake of transferring all of mom's money into bonds, money market funds, and guaranteed investment contracts (GICs) at this time, because she still needs some capital growth to stay ahead of inflation, and, as a rule, you can get this growth only from equities.

So the best investing strategy in retirement is to assemble a conservative mix of equities, bonds, and cash vehicles that produces enough income to live on but also grows in value over time. This might mean keeping about 60 percent of mom's assets in cash instruments, like money-market funds, and fixed-income assets, such as Treasury, high-quality corporate, junk, and municipal bonds; mortgage-backed securities; fixed annuities; and the mutual funds that hold these assets.

Invest the remaining 20 percent of mom's money in stocks or stock mutual funds, which provide an inflation hedge. Most of these stocks and funds should be high yielding so they give her current income, as well as growth. To find safer, high-yielding stocks, search such industries as electric, gas, water, and telephone utilities; banking; oil; and insurance. If your mom's the type and can afford to take a risk, and would like to have a bit of fun, she might want to invest a small portion of her portfolio—perhaps 10 percent—in more growth-oriented stocks or stock funds. She must be prepared to lose some or a good portion of this money, or she should not do it at all. Focus on a diversified portfolio of mutual funds holding mostly high-yielding stocks. Types of funds she might want in her portfolio that offer growth potential and current income include total return, balanced, equity-income, growth and income, and convertible funds. She can buy such funds in either open-end or closed-end form.

As the value of your mother's portfolio changes over time, it should be rebalanced to keep a proper mix of income and growth components. For example, if the stock market rises sharply, her equity portion may rise significantly beyond 40 percent. Thus, she might consider selling some of the stocks and reinvesting the money in bonds, which will produce more income. If stock prices fall, she might buy stocks at bargain prices with some of the income from her bonds.

These suggestions only broadly outline a strategy to maximize mom's assets. The precise allocation of assets at any particular time depends on personal risk tolerance, cash flow needs, tax brackets, interest rates, market prices, and the outlook for the economy.

Budget Travel: Creating a Spending Plan that Works

By now, you have assembled a pretty accurate picture of where mom stands financially. You know what her assets and liabilities are and you have analyzed how her income matches up with her expenses (to review, see Roadmaps 2.1 and 2.2). Using this information as a base, you now must project into the future to create a budget that works for her. This should be done together, if mom is able. Indeed, if you are doing this as preparation for the future, she may be able to do it herself, and you can review it together. Conversely, you may have to take on the full responsibility if she is not able to participate. She will have a better idea of those things she feels are priorities and those she's willing to do away with, if needed.

Often, the word budget sounds constricting, foreboding, and even a bit frightening, especially if your mother has never formalized the process, but it can actually be freeing. Using it as a guide, a budget will give her (or you, if necessary) control over her finances—in a way that lets her decide what is most and least important to her. If she's never done one and is reluctant to do it now, explain to her that a budget is a living, breathing document that expands or contracts as circumstances change. It is a road map that will let her know the direction she wants to go, but will give you several options on how to get there.

For example, she may want to take a trip to Greece next year. She may also want to help with her grandson's college expenses and continue living in her own home.

Analyzing her income and her expenses, she may realize that she can't do all three and will have to forgo that trip to Greece, give her grandson less, or move to a smaller home or apartment and invest the equity she has recovered to create more income. Disappointing as that may be, she'll be able to adapt her budget priorities to altered circumstances.

Once Roadmaps 2.1, 2.2, 2.3, and 2.4 have been completed, you and mom will be able to answer the key question: Based on current assets, liabilities, income and expenses, does mom have enough money to live comfortably for the rest of her life; if not, what changes must she (or you) make? Many such questions will continue to arise as your mother moves through different stages of her life, and together you and she will be in a position to make rational, informed decisions based on the budget information in Roadmaps 2.5 and 2.6 which are annual and monthly budget worksheets.

Creating a written budget accomplishes several tasks: It communicates priorities in black and white when they may have been communicated only verbally in the past. The process of creating a budget may, in itself, motivate mom (and you, if needed) to take charge of her financial life. As the year goes on, she will feel in control of her money because she will know whether she's spending more or less than she expected. And at the end of the year or more often if desired, she will be able to evaluate how she did.

As you make out mom's annual budget (see Roadmap 2.5), keep in mind a few commonsense tips:

1. A budget takes thought, and may initially create stress for your mother, so you probably can't do a good job of forecasting all her income and expenses in an afternoon. Plan to do it in several sessions over about a week's time.
2. Do your first few rounds of budgeting in pencil so you can erase until all the numbers add up.
3. Help mom to be realistic and specific about her situation. Neither of you should count on wishful levels of spending or income. That will only frustrate the exercise. Also, remember that a budget, in itself, will not increase mom's income or cut her spending; it only allows each of you to see what is going on so it can be improved.
4. Use round numbers. You're not trying to drive yourself or mom crazy. When making projections for the next year, don't automatically assume mom will receive or spend the same amount in each category as she did the previous year. Last year's figures should be a guide, not a straitjacket. Part of the goal of budgeting is for mom to take control of her finances, so move numbers on the expense side up or down, depending—to some extent—on what she would like to see happen in the next year.

In setting up mom's budget (see Roadmap 2.5), use the totals from Roadmap 2.4. In the first column, Actual Last Year, record your mother's actual income and expenditures in each of the categories. This should be easy because all you have to do is transfer the figures from the Cash Flow Worksheet.

Next, in the Budget This Year column, you want to estimate her income and what she plans to spend in each of the categories over the next year. As she proceeds through the year, she will be keeping track of what she is actually taking in and spending in each category. This should be entered in the

third column, Actual This Year. In the fourth column, calculate whether she is above or below what she projected in each category. Label this last column, (+/–)Budget vs. Actual This Year or Difference.

With this design, you and she can instantly see whether her income and expenses are coming in over or under projections. When you total them, you can observe whether she is shooting above or below the total budget. If she is over budget, the culprit category usually sticks out like a sore thumb. If she is under budget, you might make a mid-course correction to see where else she can put some money, such as in savings or investments.

In addition to doing an annual budget, she should keep a running tab of how she is doing on a monthly basis—at least in the major categories. The Monthly Budgeting Worksheet in Roadmap 2.6 will let her compare her budgeted amount with her actual income and spending. At the end of the worksheet, she will be able to calculate whether she is over or under budget overall. Using this worksheet, she will be able to see month by month what kind of progress she is making toward meeting her budget and what items are at the greatest variance with her projections.

▶ Bump in the Road: When Your Parent's Income Isn't Enough

Your dad, like many seniors, may well be sitting on a large pool of untapped cash—his home. Many seniors are house rich and cash poor. They've paid off —or nearly paid off—their mortgages, maintained their homes, and, over the years, may well have seen the value of their property multiply exponentially. Yet, many of them can't make ends meet on their Social Security income, and have no extra funds for home repairs or emergencies, let alone to enjoy their retirement or spend their golden years worry-free.

Moving On: Selling the Family Home

One way to boost dad's retirement income is to cash in on the value he has built up in his home. He may want to sell the home and buy a smaller one or rent an apartment that will cost less and be easier to maintain (more on these options in Chapter 3). Unless he has made a profit of over $250,000, he will not owe taxes on it as long as it is his primary residence, which is defined as a home in which you lived for at least two of the past five years. (You can sell your primary residence every two years and take advantage of this rule.) There is no requirement that you reinvest your home sale proceeds in another house, so he can rent another home and invest the proceeds in stocks, bonds, mutual funds, annuities, and other investments that will pay him a regular income.

> *Married couples filing jointly can avoid all capital gains when selling their primary residence if their profit is $500,000 or less. If you are single, you avoid all capital gains taxes if your profit is $250,000 or less.*

When the time comes to sell dad's home, he (and you) must do a bit of homework. The first step in getting the highest price possible is to obtain a realistic appraisal of its current value. If he has paid little attention to the market, and you are unfamiliar with it, your sense of what his home is worth may be outdated. You can get a feel for the market by scanning newspaper ads for similar properties and by visiting nearby open houses. Real estate agents will be glad to give you and dad a free assessment of his home's strengths, weaknesses, and fair price range. For a fee, you can also obtain a professional appraiser's opinion. If you want to avoid the real estate broker's fee, you can try to sell his home on your own with newspaper ads and a "For Sale" sign on the front lawn. Although you and he will have to deal with browsers and people unqualified to buy the property, you may be lucky enough to find someone who falls in love with the home and places a bid on it.

Before you let anyone past the front door, make sure dad's home is in tip-top shape. Add a fresh coat of paint. Locate plants and flowers strategically. Mow the lawn. Spruce up the exterior. Clean every room thoroughly. Remove excess clutter and furniture to maximize the appearance of living space. Distribute a one-page fact sheet listing the home's selling points and illustrating the layout. If dad's home is located in an active real estate market, you might be able to sell within a few weeks. If at all possible, sell dad's home before he buys or rents another. You don't want him to be responsible for the costs if his home sells more slowly than anticipated.

If you cannot sell dad's home on your own, bring in several real estate agents to compete for your listing. Unless you deal with a flat-fee or discount broker, you must pay the agent you choose a commission of 6 percent to 7

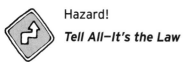

Hazard!
Tell All—It's the Law

More and more states require that you disclose all of your home's problems in writing to prospective buyers. The document covers a property's structure, utilities (such as plumbing, air-conditioning, and water system), and municipal status (such as building permits, zoning restrictions, certificate of occupancy, and property tax rates). If the buyer signs this sales disclosure form acknowledging that they have been informed of the home's problems, the buyer has little right to sue you later if any problems crop up for any of the items listed.

If you are not familiar with the house or what's been going on around town and dad is unable to give you this information, it may pay to have a professional look the place over and to check with neighbors and real estate agents about what's going on around town. It might even pay to do a search of the local papers or check in at the town hall.

percent of your home's selling price, but if the agent can find a buyer when you can't or they can get a better net price, the fee is worthwhile.

When you sell dad's home, either on your own or through an agent, you must deduct all selling and closing costs from the gross sales price to arrive at dad's net proceeds. The Roadmap 2.7 lists some of the costs you might incur and helps you determine your profit.

Funding a Get-Away: Refinancing and Reverse Mortgages

Dad doesn't have to move or sell his home to cash in on it, however. He can get a reverse mortgage. In the past, the only ways seniors had to tap the equity in their homes were to refinance the home, which is difficult unless you can show the ability to make the payments, or to sell and move to something less expensive. Reverse mortgages, also known as a home-equity conversion, in which a lender—such as a bank or thrift—makes a loan against the value of your home and sends you a monthly check for as long as you live in the residence, present a third possibility.

How much you get depends on your life expectancy, the amount of equity in your home and the interest rate charged by the lender. When you die

Roadmap 2.7

Net Proceeds Worksheet

	$ Amount	Total
Gross Equity		
Sale Price of Property	_____	
Minus Remaining Mortgage Balance	(_____)	
Minus Other Home-Related Debts	(_____)	
Total gross equity		$_____
Selling and Closing Costs		
Escrow or Other Fees	$_____	
Legal and Document Preparation Fees	_____	
Title Search and Insurance Fees	_____	
Transfer Taxes	_____	
FHA, VA, or Lender Discounts	_____	
Mortgage Prepayment Penalties	_____	
Real Estate Taxes Owed	_____	
Appraisal Fees	_____	
Survey Fees	_____	
Termite and Other Pest Inspection Fees	_____	
Fees for Repair Work Required by Sales Contract	_____	
Home Protection or Warranty Plan Fees	_____	
Unpaid Assessments	_____	
Real Estate Commissions	_____	
Other Selling or Closing Costs	_____	
Total selling and closing costs		$_____
Total gross equity minus		$_____
Total selling and closing costs equals		(_____)
Net proceeds		$_____

or move to another home, the lender usually takes title to the property and sells it to pay off the loan balance. Before you decide to take this route, however, you and dad should consider the alternatives.

Look at All Your Options. Do you or your dad know what his house is worth? Do you know the cost of buying or renting a new home? Have you looked into the cost and feasibility of moving into an apartment, an assisted-living facility, or other alternative housing? Do you know if dad wants to stay in his own home? Many seniors do, but don't just assume that your parent will. After all, your dad might be glad not to have to worry about snow removal or mowing the lawn or fixing the furnace! Or he might be unable to think of the alternatives. If he does, have you examined the possibility of taking in a roommate or adding on to the house to create an apartment to provide rental income? (More on this and related possibilities in Chapter 3.)

Are there other sources of money you and he haven't considered? Is dad eligible for Supplemental Security Income (SSI) or other assistance programs (see the previous section)? Could he qualify and make the payments on a low-cost home equity loan? Before considering any type of major refinancing (including a reverse mortgage) or selling your home, review these and other possibilities.

Refinancing. Even if dad does not have a fully paid-up mortgage because he refinanced his home along the way, it's possible that he locked himself into what he thought was a good fixed-rate mortgage, but if rates have since dropped, he may want to consider refinancing the loan to save what could total thousands of dollars over the long term. What is much more important at this stage in his life is to gain access to any additional equity that has built up over the years since he last refinanced.

The rule of thumb in the industry used to be that your new mortgage had to be at least two percentage points less than your existing mortgage for the transaction to be worthwhile. Recently, however, the competition among lenders has shaved closing costs significantly, and in many cases, it might pay to refinance if the difference is one percentage point or possibly even less. It all depends on how much the new lender charges in closing costs, and how long dad plans to stay in his home. (You and he must realistically assess his situation in terms of his longevity and his health as well as his family's medical history.)

It only makes sense to refinance if dad's home has enough value to justify a new loan. Most lenders will make you go through the same application process when you refinance as you did when you applied for your original mortgage. You must again pay loan origination fees, credit report charges, appraisal charges, inspection fees, points, mortgage recording taxes, title insurance, and legal fees. Before dad refinances, he should also determine whether his current loan, if any, imposes prepayment penalties. If so, refinancing can be significantly more expensive.

To determine whether dad should refinance his current mortgage, calculate his refinancing costs; then complete the Refinancing Worksheet in Roadmap 2.8. Sample figures are provided. In the example in Roadmap 2.8 it would take the borrower 10 months of lower payments to recover the $3,000 in up-front refinancing costs. Therefore, the borrower must stay in the home at least 10 months after the refinancing to see any savings. In other cases, the savings would be less and the payback period would be longer. Again, it is worthwhile to refinance *only* if dad will live in his house for a significant amount of time after he refinances.

When you refinance, he will pay less interest on the new loan. That saves him money, but it means that he will receive fewer mortgage interest deductions to lower his tax bill (on the other hand, he is probably doing this because he needs the cash and doesn't have much taxable income anyway). Also, any points he pays on a refinance can be deducted only over the life of the loan, not up front in a lump sum.

A good way to determine whether refinancing makes sense and what refinancing options are best for dad is to analyze his situation using calculators available on numerous Web sites (see Appendix B: Resources). If the math indicates refinancing, try dad's existing lender first. In order to keep his business, it will probably give him a competitive deal and might even waive certain procedures or fees, such as the appraisal or prepayment charges. Still, before he recommits to his lender, shop around for other lenders to see whether he can obtain an even better deal.

Depending on the size of the mortgage, dad will have to meet income requirements. Before you apply, do the calculations to see if he will qualify. If he doesn't, consider selling or the reverse mortgage option.

How Reverse Mortgages Work. This mortgage allows homeowners, age 62 and up, to borrow against their home's value and receive a lump sum,

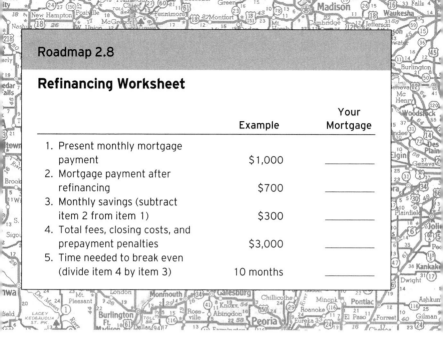

Roadmap 2.8

Refinancing Worksheet

	Example	Your Mortgage
1. Present monthly mortgage payment	$1,000	_____
2. Mortgage payment after refinancing	$700	_____
3. Monthly savings (subtract item 2 from item 1)	$300	_____
4. Total fees, closing costs, and prepayment penalties	$3,000	_____
5. Time needed to break even (divide item 4 by item 3)	10 months	_____

monthly cash advances, or advances from a credit line. No income is required because no payment is made until the borrowers die, sell their home, or permanently move out. In the meantime, the monthly interest is added to the amount(s) borrowed.

Generally, the older you are, the more you can borrow, and the greater the appraisal of your house, the higher the loan. However, the National Housing Act, section 203-b, has mandated county-by-county limits.

What this means is that instead of borrowing against your equity and paying interest, you contract with a bank to convert some of your home equity to cash while you retain ownership. On a regular mortgage, each monthly payment increases your equity and lowers the loan balance. With a reverse mortgage, the amount owed increases each month and the equity decreases. (Of course, if the homes where dad lives are appreciating, that will add to his equity, since he still owns the home.) With a reverse mortgage, you remain the homeowner. You are still responsible for insurance, taxes, and upkeep. And, while you cannot be foreclosed, failure to keep the property up or pay taxes could trigger default on your reverse mortgage.

Dad can take the proceeds of a reverse mortgage in a lump sum, in monthly checks, or through a line of credit he can tap whenever he wants. He can also use the money for anything he wants, but of course it is prudent to use it for living expenses such as taxes, insurance, heat, food, or health care.

Different Types of Reverse Mortgages. The Home Equity Conversion Mortgage (HECM) is the only reverse mortgage insured by the federal government (through the Federal Housing Administration [FHA]). Unless you qualify for a specialized state or local government loan as discussed below, the HECM program is usually the best consumer option for reverse mortgages.

The FHA stipulates to HECM lenders how much you can borrow, based on your age and home value. The HECM program holds down loan costs, which can be substantial. And the FHA ensures that lenders meet all their obligations. As a general rule, HECM programs provide the largest loan advances and the most payout options.

There are three basic types of reverse mortgages from which to choose:

1. FHA-insured. You need not pay off an FHA-insured reverse mortgage as long as you live in your home. You can change your payment options from monthly advances to a line of credit at any time at little or no cost. The FHA guarantees your payments even if the lender defaults.
2. Lender-insured. A lender-insured plan generally offers a heftier line of credit or larger monthly payments than an FHA-insured plan. Also, you do not have to borrow against the full equity in your home, as you do with an FHA-insured loan. Often, however, a lender-insured loan imposes a number of higher costs, which means that your loan balance will grow quickly, leaving you with less equity. Compare such a loan carefully with its HECM counterpart. For help, visit http://www.hud. gov/offices/hsg/sfh/hecm/hecm--df.cfm
3. Uninsured. An uninsured plan pays a fixed monthly payment for a certain number of years—which you choose when you open the line —then terminates. At that point, the loan balance comes due, and the lender may take title to your home. An uninsured plan usually charges a fixed interest rate and requires no mortgage insurance. The plan can work well if you know how long you will need payments. But if you run through the equity in your home and still need more money, you will likely lose your home to an uninsured lender.

Many states and localities offer targeted versions of reverse mortgages that should be considered. Deferred Payment Loans (DPLs) provide a single lump sum payment to improve or repair your home. Property Tax Deferrals (PTDs) provide annual loan advances just to pay property taxes.

A related way for dad to tap into his home's equity is to assume a Reverse Annuity Mortgage (RAM). With this plan, you use the proceeds generated by a mortgage on your home to buy an annuity from an insurance company. The insurer pays the interest on your mortgage and sends the rest of the money to you in monthly installments. Upon your death, the insurer usually sells your home and repays the mortgage balance. Remaining funds are passed on to your heirs through your estate.

The amount of monthly income dad would receive from a RAM depends on the interest rate the insurer pays, his life expectancy, and the equity he has accumulated in his home. Because the insurance company risks that dad will live longer than its actuarial tables predict, the insurer makes smaller monthly payments than dad might receive through a traditional reverse mortgage.

1. Closing costs. Money from the reverse mortgage can pay closing costs, which are added to the loan and paid back at the end of the loan. There is an origination fee, up to 2 percent of the home's value or the county's 203-b limit. For smaller loans, lenders are allowed to charge up to $2,000. These costs are sometimes negotiable, so it pays to shop around.

    Other costs include title search and insurance, appraisal fees, credit checks, and the like. Because the up-front costs are heavy, reverse mortgages make the most sense if your parent plans to stay in the home for a long time. So, ask yourselves if dad will be healthy enough to live in the house alone or with a caregiver, assuming that's an option, for a good long time.

2. All HECM reverse mortgage products (and most others) have a cap or non-recourse limit, which means that even if the prices of houses fall after dad receives the loan, he or his heirs only have to repay the amount he receives for the house when it is sold. For example, if dad's house is worth $175,000 and his reverse mortgage loan balance is $200,000, the lender can only collect $175,000. This feature is paid for through a Mortgage Insurance Premium (MIP) which costs 2 percent of the home's value and .5 percent added to your interest rate. The Mortgage Insurance Premium also ensures that you will receive the promised loan advances and will not have to repay the loan for as long as dad stays in the home.

3. Some reverse mortgage loans charge a fixed rate of interest, while others charge a variable rate. Over time, the interest owed can become considerable, and your equity stake can shrink dramatically unless housing prices rise significantly. However, a reverse mortgage can be a good way to use the equity in dad's home.

4. All payments you receive from a reverse mortgage (technically, they are loan advances) are considered nontaxable income. Therefore, they do not lower dad's Social Security or Medicaid benefits. On the other hand, the interest he pays on the reverse mortgage is not tax deductible until he pays off all or part of the total reverse mortgage debt.

Reverse mortgages are complex, and even to qualify for an FHA-insured HECM, you must discuss the loan, free of charge, with an FHA-approved counselor. For more information, call 800-569-4287.

A Trip to a Casino: Cashing in on Life Insurance

In addition to providing death benefits, life insurance also can offer living benefits. If your parent owns a whole life or universal life insurance policy, he may now be able to tap into it for supplemental retirement income depending upon how much equity he has built up in the policy.

If dad has life insurance and has been diagnosed as terminally ill, and is desperately in need of money, one option may be to sell the policy to a viatical settlement provider.

When you sell a life insurance policy to a viatical settlement company, in exchange for all the rights and obligations under your life insurance policy, you receive a lump-sum cash payment that is a percentage of the face value of your policy (usually 40 to 85 percent). The settlement company can then sell the policy to a third party who buys it as an investment. The investor makes money on the difference between the policy's face value and the amount you will receive. The investor continues to pay the premiums on the policy until your parent dies and the policy's benefits are paid to the investor.

In general, if your parent is terminally ill, the amount your parent will receive is not subject to federal income tax. If the diagnosis were chronically ill, then the settlement would also not be subject to federal income tax, as long as the funds are used to pay for long-term care services.

Eligibility for Viatical Settlements. Each viatical settlement company sets its own rules for determining which life insurance policies it will buy. Most viatical companies will require that:

▶ You have owned your policy for at least two years.
▶ Your current beneficiary signs a release or a waiver.
▶ You are terminally ill (some companies require a life expectancy of two years or less, while others may buy your policy even if your life expectancy is four years).
▶ You sign a release allowing the viatical settlement provider access to your medical records.

If an employer provides your parent's life insurance policy, purchasers will want to know if it can be converted into an individual policy or otherwise be guaranteed to remain in force.

How to Choose a Viatical Settlement Provider. In most states, viatical settlement providers must be registered or licensed by the department of insurance to do business. Some states forbid the practice of selling viatical settlements. The National Association of Insurance Commissioners' Web site (http://www.naic.org/state_contacts) can help you find licensed settlement providers in your area. You can also find out if there are any complaints or fraud cases pending against a viatical settlement company.

Here are a few things to keep in mind if you're shopping for a viatical settlement.

1. Contact two or three viatical settlement companies and compare their discounts. Generally speaking, the shorter the person's life expectancy, the greater percentage of the face value of the policy you should receive.
2. Check with your state insurance department to see if viatical settlement companies and their brokers must be licensed and if the company your dad is considering is in good standing with your state's insurance commission.
3. Do not fall for high-pressure sales tactics and too-good-to-be-true promises. Make sure that the viatical settlement company has the money for dad's payout readily available. Insist that the company set up an escrow account with a reputable, independent, third-party financial institution to deposit the funds used for your offer. Do not sign any paperwork until

the money is in the escrow account. Insist on a timely payment. Once the life insurance company has completed its work, dad should get the money from the escrow agent in two to three business days.

4. Ask about privacy. Potential investors can make a decision about your viatical case without your name and personal information.

5. Consult an attorney to discuss possible probate and estate considerations.

Since complex legal and financial matters are involved, viatical settlement transactions require time. Your parent's physician as well as the insurance company and financial advisors will also be involved. Sometimes the entire process can run up to four months or longer. You and your parent may wish to consider these options, if available:

1. Use any accumulated cash value already in the life insurance policy (if it is a whole life, universal life, or variable life policy).

2. Borrow money from the beneficiary(s) of the policy. The money they lend you is repaid when they receive the death benefit.

3. Some life insurance companies offer "accelerated death benefits" directly in return for increased premium payments or a reduced final death benefit to the original beneficiary.

4. If your dad has other financial assets, such as equity investments, sell them or liquidate retirement accounts. While this approach may sound drastic, when you do the math, you may find that dad comes out further ahead with this strategy.

This is clearly a last resort option. Should the time come that you and your parent consider it, there will no doubt be many things weighing heavily on your mind—and you may feel that you do not have the time or energy to focus on financial matters. For this reason, if it seems you might one day need to consider this option, you should take the time now to educate yourself regarding all your alternatives.

The choices that you and your parent make about these life insurance benefits can affect the people they love. Before any decisions about a viatical settlement are made, talk it over with your family and friends as well as a reliable third party who has no financial stake in the decision such as a lawyer, an accountant, or a financial planner.

Finding a Comfortable Berth

Choosing the Right Place to Live

For most of us, the change from an active work life to retirement also suggests a major change of lifestyle. As we age, there are changes in our physical abilities and the retirement home should meet those new requirements. As part of your parents' retirement plans, they might consider moving to a new area or to a smaller, less demanding home or renovating their current home.

If they have done everything right and have set up a reliable stream of retirement income, they still must decide on the lifestyle they want to live in their golden years. Considering and deciding on the present and long-term housing alternatives should be an essential part of that planning. Deciding where they want to live as they grow older is among the most important decisions they must make. Finance, of course, is an important aspect, but they should consider other factors as well; for example, what if one or both of them become ill; what will happen when one dies? Do they want to plan for those eventualities or are they willing and able to make another move?

In this chapter, we are going to assume that your parents are about to or have retired and are in the process of making the decision about their living arrangements. It is our hope that they will include you at the outset, so that you can be involved in their decision-making process. In the process, you will also realize the options available down the road when either one or both require your assistance.

▶ Armchair Travel: Adapting the Family Home to Changing Needs

There really is no place like home. When asked about their preference for housing, most seniors answer, "What l would really like to do is to stay right here." For most Americans, their own home symbolizes security and independence.

Most housing, however, is designed for young, active, and mobile people. To live at home, a person must, at the very least, have access to transportation, go shopping, cook, and do household chores. Many of us will lose one or more of these abilities as we grow older.

One option, assuming your parents can afford it, is to purchase in home services, to cope with declining abilities. For a fee, an army of workers will appear to cut your grass, wash your windows, cook your meals, do the shopping, and even provide personal care and/or skilled nursing care. This may be the option, depending on the amount of help they need.

Assuming your parents have decided to make the family home their retirement castle, there are some other things that they and you should consider to make their home safer and more comfortable for them as they age. For example, some simple modifications and repairs can make it easier and safer to carry out activities such as bathing, cooking, and climbing stairs while some alterations to the physical structure of the home can improve its overall safety and condition. Not all of these things have to be done and certainly all of them do not have to be done immediately, but you and they should bear them in mind.

Research suggests that one-third to one-half of home accidents can be prevented by modification and repair that can allow people to remain in their homes. Older people tend to live in older homes that often need repairs and modifications. Over 60 percent of older persons live in homes more than 20 years old.

Sharing Your Berth: Accessory Apartment or a Home Within a Home

Another option you may want to consider if your parent, especially one who has been widow(er)ed, wants to remain in the family home is taking in a boarder, who would share the home much as youngsters do when they find a roommate to share an apartment. This would help with some of the expenses;

depending on your parent's desires, provide companionship; and, last but not necessarily least, assist with the chores around the house. There are several ways in which this can be accomplished by:

▶ sharing the living areas of the house; each person having a separate bedroom

▶ creating a separate apartment; in some homes, this can be accomplished relatively simply and with minimal expense; in others this can be a costly option

If you decide to go the route of creating a separate apartment, before you begin check zoning and other local ordinances to make certain that you are able to do this in your community.

You, especially your parent, should carefully consider with whom to share their home. Maybe you and your family could move in with mom and dad or vice versa. In some families an adult child or grandchild or other family friend or relation is the obvious choice; in others this is not feasible.

Some older people enjoy having a younger person around the house. If this is something mom would enjoy, consider contacting local colleges and universities. My mother-in-law shared her apartment with a stream of medical students from China who were studying in the U.S. for two years. This worked extremely well for her. Others prefer the companionship of someone their own age; still others want to keep it "strictly business." Perhaps a young couple, new to the community, might be the solution. Perhaps in exchange for chores like shopping, cooking, cleaning, or yard work, or other things, you could devise an exchange in lieu of rent (or some of the rent). Talk about these options and explore with mom what would be best for her. (These discussions may tell her that sharing with a stranger, or anyone, is not an option.) Whatever she decides, the initial arrangement should be on a "trial" basis, say a few weeks or a month, to see if it suits her.

Where Does Your Parent Want to Go? Determining Where to Live

Although most people remain in the homes they lived in while working, many retirees move to a warmer climate or a town that imposes less of a tax burden. While the lure of a warm and possibly faraway place and fresh start may be appealing in theory, your parents should think through such a decision carefully (if your parent is a widow(er), this is an even more im-

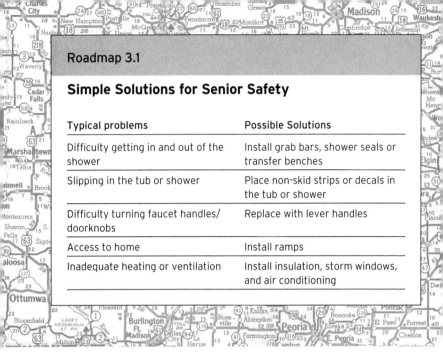

Roadmap 3.1

Simple Solutions for Senior Safety

Typical problems	Possible Solutions
Difficulty getting in and out of the shower	Install grab bars, shower seals or transfer benches
Slipping in the tub or shower	Place non-skid strips or decals in the tub or shower
Difficulty turning faucet handles/doorknobs	Replace with lever handles
Access to home	Install ramps
Inadequate heating or ventilation	Install insulation, storm windows, and air conditioning

portant decision because they'd be on their own). Assuming both parents are in good health now, the ultimate choice should be theirs. But, as we said, as this trip progresses it will help both you and them if the decisions were made in consultation with you.

If they are moving outside their present community, in addition to their financial situation or the state of their health, they should also consider the intangibles. For example, it can be difficult to put down new roots at a stage in their lives when they might want to relax. Moving far from children, grandchildren, close friends, and relatives means that they will see them less. Will this be a problem for them? They will also have to replace their entire network of professionals, from doctors and plumbers to financial planners. They might make this transition easily and thrive in their new setting.

Perhaps, most important, they must ask themselves, what would happen if one of us became incapacitated or died? Would I want to live here; how difficult would it be to relocate? If you are the person responsible for the care of your parents, how would this affect you and your family—financially, physically, emotionally?

Assuming the decision is still to move out of the area, you can help your parents reach a decision by consulting one of the guidebooks that rate retirement communities. Wherever they choose to go, unless it's in the same community in which they now live or one they have experienced over a period of time, it is a good idea to rent in the new place for a few months to make sure that they like it before selling their home and moving there. They do not want to go through the ordeal of selling their home of many years and moving all their possessions to a new place, only to discover that they don't like living there after all.

Globetrotting: Moving Overseas

For the most adventurous retirees, a move to a foreign country may make sense—at least while your parents are active and in good health.

The U.S. dollar goes much further in many other countries than it does at home. If your parents are toying with the idea they might find an enclave of retired Americans in a foreign land, which will make them feel almost like living in the States. The countries with the largest concentrations of expatriate Americans are Mexico, Canada, Italy, the Philippines, Greece, Germany, Great Britain, and Israel.

If your parents are thinking of retiring abroad, make certain they evaluate the political stability of the country, as well as the exchange rate for the dollar (but again, keep it mind it will fluctuate). Some developing countries like Mexico and the Philippines offer a lower cost of living, while industrialized nations like Great Britain and Germany are far more expensive.

They should also inquire about their tax obligations if they move abroad. As long as they remain U.S. citizens, they owe U.S. taxes. In some countries, you must pay local income tax as well. Usually, you can claim a foreign tax credit on your U.S. return to offset those local taxes. They should also look into health insurance coverage because it is unlikely that Medicare will cover them if they live abroad.

▶ Fork in the Road: Buying vs. Renting

Having made the decision to sell the family home, the first question your parents must ask themselves in deciding where to live is whether to buy or rent. The following factors will help them make an informed decision. (Again, we're assuming finances and health are good and the future prospect is sunny.)

Roadmap 3.2

Questions to Ask Before Moving

Assuming your parents want to move—whether near or far—they should consider the following factors as they evaluate potential locations. They are not listed in any particular order of importance, because everyone has different priorities. Research, think through, and discuss each.

The Community

1. What size is the community? Does it have your preferred daily atmosphere?

2. How available is public transportation, if and when you no longer drive?

3. What is its proximity to airports, bus service, and train stations, if travel is in your retirement plans?

4. Are community centers, activities, libraries, and theaters readily available?

5. Is the community senior-friendly? What senior programs, educational programs, assisted-living facilities, and home health care agencies are in place; and how well-funded are they?

6. Is it close to family and/or friends? Will family easily be able to visit you?

7. How easy will it be to make new friends in this community?

8. What's the community's tax base? How much are the current state and local income taxes?

9. Are the estate tax rules the same as in the state from which you are moving? Better? Worse?

10. What's the median age? A youthful community may have more demands for school growth and funding issues. Will other services be sacrificed?

11. Look at the crime statistics for the area. Has there been a significant change in the past five years?

12. What's the weather like?

13. How close is shopping for food, clothes, gasoline and auto repairs, pharmacy needs, household items, gifts, and more? How far do you want to travel for regular grocery needs?

14. Do you have banking choices?

15. Is there public and private mail and package delivery?

16. How far do you have to travel for fun and entertainment outside your home?

17. What is the distance to major highways?

18. How large are nearby major cities, and how do they affect your community?

19. What community groups are active in town?

20. How far will you have to travel to worship? What is the spirit and health of the local place of worship you will most likely attend?

21. What's the diversity of the community—ethnicity, income, and age?

22. Are restaurants nearby?

23. How available are the sporting activities that you enjoy?

24. How far will you have to travel to engage in hobbies?

25. Are there educational opportunities available?

26. How close are doctors, specialists, and hospitals?

27. What long-term care facilities are in the area, and would you want to stay in any of them?

28. Do you ever want to move again?

29. What's of interest nearby when friends, family, and grandchildren stay with you?

30. What is the fire department's rating?

31. What's the availability of hotels and motels in the area?

32. How close are dry cleaning, shoe repair, a hair stylist, an accountant, and other services?

The Home

1. What size of home do you require?

2. What is the cost of housing, as well as ongoing cost of living?

3. Where will your guests stay?

4. If you enjoy entertaining, what facilities do you want in the kitchen, dining area, and outside area?

5. How old is the home, roof, paint etc.?

6. What is its proximity to many of the community items listed above?

7. Where will the grandchildren play when they visit? Can they bicycle, skateboard, and roller-skate in the neighborhood?

8. Is there space for storage, doing hobbies, etc.?

9. How close are the nearest neighbors?

Advantages of Buying

1. They will build up equity, or ownership, in their home over time as long as their home is appreciating in value. If they choose to take out a mortgage, they leverage their cash outlay.

2. If they buy right and their home is well maintained and in a good location, they have a good chance of substantial capital appreciation over time. Homes provide one of the best hedges against inflation.

3. They can remodel their home to suit their needs and tastes. They are unlikely to do so for rental property.

4. Owning a home offers a deeper sense of commitment to the community. Homeowners, wanting to maintain property values, tend to take care of their homes better than renters. They also tend to be more involved in civic issues, such as neighborhood improvement.

5. As a homeowner, they may qualify for several significant tax advantages. First, all mortgage interest they pay up to $1 million qualifies as a deduction, reducing both your federal and state income tax burdens. In addition, they can deduct any interest charged on home equity loans of up to $100,000 taken out against the value of their home. Local property taxes are also deductible from your federal income tax. If you sell your home, you do not have to pay any capital gains tax as long as you have lived in it as your principal residence for two of the previous five years, and your profit does not exceed $500,000 if you are a married couple filing taxes jointly or $250,000 if you are filing taxes as a single.

6. Their home can be a source of future cash. Whether they borrow against it through a second mortgage or a home equity loan, or pull out the cash slowly through a reverse annuity mortgage (explained in more detail in Chapter 2), they can put their equity to work for them when they need it most.

Advantages of Renting

1. The costs of home ownership, from the down payment to the monthly mortgage and maintenance costs, may take a large bite out of their household budget, although if your parents are selling an appreciated home on which they have little or no mortgage, the down payment should not be a problem. Many people sacrifice their entire lifestyle by sinking 50 percent or more of their income into home ownership costs. If they can

rent for 30 percent or less of their income, they may live a less stressful life.

2. Prices of homes may fall. By renting, they will not be hurt by eroding real estate prices.

3. By funneling the money they would be paying in mortgage payments and maintenance costs into a diversified portfolio of securities, they may be able to build up as much equity over time, since stocks, bonds, and mutual funds may rise in value faster than home prices. In addition, these assets are much more liquid than real estate, and, unlike a home, generate regular income, which your parents can reinvest. All this assumes they have the discipline to do this or a skilled financial advisor to do this for them.

4. Depending on the strength of the local rental market, they may be able to avoid rent increases or even pay below-market rent.

5. Remember, at this stage in their lives they might see a lot of changes in a relatively short time. For example, their housing needs may be different several years from now; it may make more sense to rent than to be forced to sell their home at what might be a stressful time. Unless the local real estate market is extremely active, you cannot expect enough appreciation in a year or two to compensate for the significant costs of buying and selling a home.

The buy-vs.-rent decision, therefore, should not be based only on finances but also on expectations for future lifestyle. To calculate the purely financial trade-offs, however, try one of the real estate software packages on the market or available free on the Internet. They will help your parents sort through the true value of housing tax benefits, the realistic costs of buying and maintaining a home, the alternative returns on their money if they rent, the number of years you must stay in a house for it to pay off, and other complex factors they should consider.

How to Get the Most for Your Travel Dollar

When your parents and you have completed the buy-vs.-rent analysis, they may conclude that it makes more sense to rent their housing and invest their money. If they plan to rent, the following tips can help them get the most for their money:

1. Before beginning their search for an apartment or a home to rent, refer back to Roadmap 2.6 to determine how much rent they can afford. They should be able to meet their rent plus all their other expenses comfortably. Remember, one of the main advantages of renting is that it should leave them with enough cash to save some. Clearly, that won't happen if they are saddled with too much rent. Ideally, rent (including utilities) should absorb no more than 30 percent of your gross income or 25 percent of your net income.

2. Next, hone in on a good location (see Roadmap 3.1). Before they settle on a neighborhood, tour it extensively during the day and at night, on weekdays and weekends, to get a feel for it.

3. Once they've decided on a location, look for rental homes or apartments advertised in newspapers, at real estate agents' offices, and on billboards in local supermarkets, schools, and bank lobbies. Depending on the strength of the market, they or the landlord will have to pay a fee if they find the apartment or rental home through a real estate agent. If there are few rentals in the local market, the renter usually pays the fee; if there are many apartments for rent, the landlord tends to pay the fee. However, you can avoid that cost if you deal directly with a landlord or with a renter who offers a sublease.

4. When looking at apartments or rental homes, check everything carefully. Run all the appliances and facilities, including the dishwasher, washing machine, toilet, shower, sink, stove, and waste disposal system. Also, make sure the refrigerator is in good condition and that heating and air conditioning systems work well. Inquire about parking facilities, security procedures, pest control, and grounds maintenance, if applicable. Determine which utility costs are included in and excluded from your rent. Finally, visit the property both in the day and at night to see —and even chat with—your potential neighbors and to determine the property's or neighborhood's noise level.

5. Once they have found a place that meets their needs, lock in as low a rent as possible. (Obviously, they will have much more leverage if a surplus of rentals exists.) Your landlord may ask for references from employers or past landlords. If possible, have them ready, in writing, in advance. Landlords will also require at least a month's security deposit and maybe two months' rent. In many states, landlords are required to put that

money in an escrow bank account and credit you with any interest it earns.

6. If they plan on staying in the apartment or rental home at least a year —and in this scenario, we assume they are—insist on getting a year-long lease (at minimum). Otherwise, they will rent under a tenant-at-will agreement, which means that they can leave whenever they want, but the landlord can evict them at will. If you plan to stay awhile, you should sign a renewable lease. In addition to allowing them to extend their rental, the lease gives them the right to have the landlord maintain the basic facilities in your apartment at an acceptable level. Ask the landlord whether your lease grants them the right to sublease to another renter and under what conditions they can get out of the lease before it officially terminates.

7. If there is a chance that they may want to own the apartment or rental home someday, ask the landlord whether the rent can be applied toward a down payment on the purchase of the property. Rent-to-own agreements are gaining popularity and may work to your parent's advantage if they can lock in a price now that may be profitable if real estate prices rise later. Most rent-to-own agreements do not obligate you to buy. Your parents can walk away from the purchase if their situation changes or real estate values fall.

On the other hand, if they conclude from the buy-versus-rent analysis that they should buy a home, they have a much more complex task ahead of them. They now must determine how much house they can afford, what kind of house to buy, how to find the best deal, how to make an offer that is accepted, and whether or not to finance the purchase with a mortgage or to pay in full and live mortgage free. (We're assuming here that they are paying less for the new home than they will get from the one they are selling.) Then they must determine whether they want a single family home or a condominium, co-op, or other association. They should also consider whether it should be located in a retirement community, assisted living, or long-term care community (more about these later in the chapter).

Assuming they have decided to invest some or most of the money they receive from the sale of their home, the first step they must take before they house hunt is to determine how large a mortgage they can afford. To qualify for a home loan, they must pass certain tests that all banks will impose. Therefore, they might as well apply those tests themselves before they ever meet with a banker. In summary, if they make a 10 percent down payment on a home, banks will approve a loan only if your monthly real estate obligation—which includes mortgage principal and interest payments, real estate taxes, homeowners insurance, and maintenance costs (for a cooperative or condominium)—is 28 percent or less of your gross monthly income. In addition, all of their debt should not total more than 36 percent of their gross monthly income.

▶ Exploring the Outside World: Housing Alternatives

Once your parents have decided to sell the family home, chosen where they want to live, and determined what price they will pay for a home, it's time to establish what kind of housing will best serve their needs, both today and in the future.

We've already discussed the things that go into choosing *where* to live; now they must decide *how* to live. What size home suits their present and future needs? Often retirees and other older people decide to move because their large home was a burden to maintain and/or too expensive to maintain. On the other hand, they've become accustomed to having space, so they must try to establish how much space they realistically need (again, refer to the questions in Roadmap 3.1).

Traveling Alone or with a Group: A Home for a New Lifestyle

Next, they must assess what type of home best suits their lifestyle. For instance, would they rather own a new home, which may offer many modern conveniences, or an older home, which they may find more charming, though less energy efficient, perhaps more in need of repair and more difficult to maintain? Finally, would they prefer to purchase an apartment in a cooperative or condominium building? Perhaps they would prefer a townhouse.

In a cooperative, they actually buy shares in the entire property, which grants them a proprietary lease to occupy an apartment. Condominiums allow them to buy the property outright. In many cases, the cooperative or condominium board of directors must approve anyone to whom they want to sell the apartment, which can make the property difficult to sell. Both coops and condos assess a monthly maintenance charge to pay for such shared costs as the property's underlying mortgage, heat, elevators, electricity, grounds maintenance, security, and recreational facilities, such as swimming pools, golf, and tennis courts. If the coop or condo must undertake a particularly large repair job, like replacing a roof or boiler, they may have to pay an extra assessment to cover their share of the bill.

Living in a well-run coop or condo can liberate your parents from much of the maintenance of a single-family home. On the other hand, it's essential to make sure that the board of directors runs the organization well. If the board continually defers essential maintenance, for example, the value of the unit could erode.

Alternative Travel Options: Living Arrangements to Suit Every Need

In addition to a traditional single family home, condo, or town home, there are a wide variety of other options to suit your parents' diverse needs as they age. As you and your parents begin to explore the options, the choices may at first be overwhelming. However, the task of choosing the right retirement community becomes much simpler when they understand the various options. You may hear about "board and care homes," "personal care homes," "life care" and "continuing care retirement facilities." All refer to some type of "assisted living" or service-oriented housing.

Among the things you and your parents should consider are their age, health, marriage and financial status, religious preference, personal interests, and hobbies, which will help them select the living arrangement that best meets their interests and needs.

Retirement Community. For older people, but especially if your parent is widow(er)ed or divorced, and living on their own, a cooperative, condominium, or town home—in a retirement community (also known as an independent living facility)—could well be the ideal choice. These communities are designed for seniors who are relatively independent both physically and socially. The major benefit of this type of arrangement is its maintenance-free living with others of the same age and with similar interests. Activities conveniently planned and carried out in independent living settings often include crafts, exercise classes, live entertainment, movies, parties, outings and overnight bus trips, each adding a new dimension to your parent's experience. Other maintenance-free amenities include trash pickup, transportation to shopping areas, and so on.

Senior Apartments. Senior apartments are a good choice for older adults who can take care of themselves. Usually, these apartments are developed like standard apartments, but differ in that they have an age restriction. Some apartments are also equipped with assistive technology such as hand rails and pull cords to aid you. Overall these apartments are great if you're looking for a community of elderly neighbors without the hassles of a larger home to manage. Some of these facilities even provide linen service and noon meals served in a common dining area. Residents generally choose apartments from one of three floor plans, and have the option of bringing their own furniture or purchasing what the facility may offer in its display rooms.

When Money Is an Issue. In addition to private independent living facilities, designed for seniors, there are also government-subsidized housing developments designed for retirees in good health who need minimum assistance. If your parents earn a low income and want to live out their retirement in a house, there is a way to do so. The U.S. government often classifies these as elderly housing and the Department of Housing and Urban Development has several programs designed to make them more affordable. (The Department of Housing and Urban Development offers information on its Web site [http://www.hud.gov/groups/seniors.cfm] and referrals to counselors who can help your parents determine what's available and what, if any, benefits they may be entitled to.)

Manufactured Home Park. If your parents own a mobile home, they can move it to a retirement-oriented park, where they pay rent and a service fee for electricity, water, and recreational facilities. In some cases, retirees band together and run such parks as nonprofit cooperatives, in which each resident owns a share of the corporation that owns the park.

Assisted Living or Continuing Care Community. Assisted living communities are designed for individuals who cannot function in an independent living environment, but do not need nursing care on a daily basis. Assisted living communities usually offer help with bathing, dressing, meals, and housekeeping.

The amount of help provided depends on individual need. Many assisted living facilities also have professional nurses and other health care professionals on staff or available on call should a resident require special care. Medicaid and Medicare cover some long-term care offered by assisted living, and some assisted living communities offer subsidies or other forms of financial aid on the basis of individual need. It provides a home in which their medical as well as general needs are managed for them.

What Are Assisted Living Residences?

1. Housing environments which provide individualized health and personal care assistance in a home-like setting. The level of care available is between that provided in congregate housing (housing with meal service) and a skilled nursing facility. In these settings:

   ▶ residents are semi-independent physically or mentally, or frail persons who need frequent assistance;

   ▶ services offered include personal care assistance, health care monitoring, limited health care services and/or the dispensing of medications;

   ▶ state licensing and regulation by state social welfare agencies is required.

2. They are important because they promote independence by meeting residents' supportive needs while preventing inappropriate institutionalization.

3. They are known by various other names. The most common are: personal care homes, sheltered housing, residential care, homes for adults, managed care, catered living, board and care, and domiciliary care.

Who Resides In Assisted Living Residences?

If your parents have difficulty performing daily tasks and have no one to help (often after one spouse dies, the other has greater difficulty functioning than when they were a couple), assisted living may be right for them. This form of housing may be appropriate if your parent needs

▶ help preparing meals, bathing, dressing, toileting, or taking medication

▶ assistance with housekeeping chores or laundry

▶ some health care assistance or monitoring

▶ transportation to doctors, shopping, and personal business, or

▶ is frequently confused or experiencing memory problems

Use Roadmap 3.3 to evaluate characteristics you should look for in an assisted living residence.

Currently most assisted living facilities are privately operated. This means that the costs of care are not usually covered by publicly financed programs. The average fee, which includes meals and personal care assistance, ranges from $1,200 to $2,000 a month. Costs are often keyed to your level of impairment and service need.

In some states, rent or service subsidies are available. However, the typical reimbursement rate provided by Supplemental Security Income (SSI) is often too low to assist those with higher levels of impairment and service needs. Your local Social Security office and Medicaid office can determine this.

Several options offer varying levels of independence combined with help with everyday living. These are available to couples as well as those on their own. The most common alternatives follow.

Congregate housing facility (Board and care homes). In such facilities, which are smaller in scale than assisted living facilities, your parents would live independently in their own apartment and share with other residents common services such as a dining room, social and recreational programs, and housekeeping. Some states will allow some nursing services to be provided, but these homes are not medical facilities and may be unlicensed. Note: Even licensed homes are infrequently monitored by the state. Make sure you inspect them carefully and check references as well as your state attorney general's office or department of consumer affairs (or equivalent) to make certain there have been no complaints against them.

Assisted-living facility. Assisted living facilities range in size from small homelike settings to large, full-scale facilities. They offer private or semi-private rooms, meals, housekeeping, and ongoing medical attention. Help with dressing, grooming, and other personal care is available. The amount of help provided depends on individual need. Many assisted living facilities also have professional nurses and other health care professionals on staff or available on call should a resident require special care. Medicaid and Medicare (see Chapter 4) cover some long-term care offered by assisted living, and some assisted living communities offer subsidies or other forms of financial aid on the basis of individual need.

Continuing-care retirement community (CCRC). A continuing care retirement community generally is a gate-secured campus designed for all stages of a retiree's life, including independent living, assisted living, and nursing home care. As their needs change, residents move from one facility

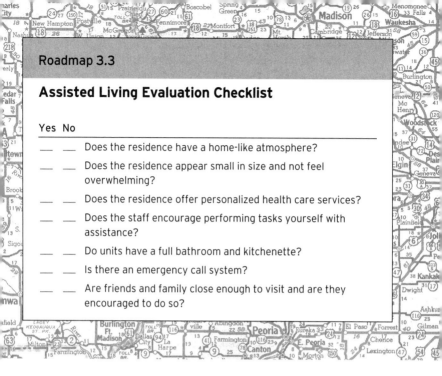

Roadmap 3.3

Assisted Living Evaluation Checklist

Yes	No	
—	—	Does the residence have a home-like atmosphere?
—	—	Does the residence appear small in size and not feel overwhelming?
—	—	Does the residence offer personalized health care services?
—	—	Does the staff encourage performing tasks yourself with assistance?
—	—	Do units have a full bathroom and kitchenette?
—	—	Is there an emergency call system?
—	—	Are friends and family close enough to visit and are they encouraged to do so?

to another within the community. People usually sign a long-term continuing-care contract with the community, which provides that the community's administrators will make sure they receive the level of aid they need as they age, essentially a continuum of housing, miscellaneous services, and health care services, commonly all on one campus. Generally, there is an entrance fee plus a regular monthly charge that covers you for as long as you live in the community. CCRC residents enjoy an independent lifestyle with the knowledge that if they become sick or frail, their needs will continue to be met. As a rule, residents are expected to move into the community while they are still independent and able to take care of themselves.

Contact the American Association of Homes and Services for the Aging for a list of continuing-care communities that are accredited by the association.

Nursing Facilities. While few opt to live in a nursing home, they are one of the most widely recognized types of housing for the elderly. They provide care for individuals who need nursing care without being in a hospital. A doctor supervises this type of care and state boards of health regulate these facilities. Nursing homes also offer short-term and respite care for those who need it.

▶ Tips for the Savvy Traveler: Evaluating the Alternatives

In evaluating any of these housing alternatives, your parents should ask themselves the following questions:

1. Does the facility offer the services they need now and are likely to need in the future?
2. Do they like the facility's location? Does it offer nearby recreational or cultural attractions?
3. What is the track record of the company running the facility? Is it financially solid? How long has it been in the business of operating retirement facilities? What is the facility's occupancy level? (An 80 percent occupancy level within a year or two of opening means that clients are satisfied.)
4. What kind of contract must they sign? They may be offered a rental agreement for a few months or years. They may have to buy the housing unit to live there. Or they may have to pay a life-use fee, which guarantees them the right to live in the facility until they die for a one-time investment of several thousand dollars as well as a monthly fee. In this case, if they move out, some of their investment may be refunded.
5. What services are available in the facility? Ask about appliances, parking, utilities, exercise and recreation classes, security, housekeeping, meals, and transportation.
6. What is the quality of medical care provided? Look into the availability of general practitioners and specialists, dentists, home health care aides, drug dispensaries, physical therapists, and psychiatric care. Ask whether the facility is certified to receive Medicare and Medicaid.
7. Does the facility accept Medicare assignment or Medicaid patients? For example, ask whether the facility accepts Medicare and your Medicare supplement as payment in full. Do you have to pay the difference between the actual charge and Medicare's allowable charge? What other fees do you have to pay? What are optional services that could add to your fees?

> *The decision about where to live is an important one and shouldn't be made hastily or without plenty of investigation.*

Finally, tour the facility extensively, and talk to as many residents as possible to learn whether they are satisfied with the condition of the facility and the level of service provided. If a residents' association or council exists, attend a meeting to get a sense of how well the facility is managed.

▶ Reinvesting the Cash

If your parents sold their home when they retired or your mom sells her home after dad dies, we assume they either bought a less expensive home or are renting an apartment. In either case, it is important that the money they received for their home is reinvested in income-producing stocks and bonds. Remember, your parents can avoid all capital gains taxes on the sale of their home as long as their profit is less than $500,000 for a married couple filing jointly or $250,000 for a single, and as long as it has been their primary residence for two of the past five years.

If your parents remain in their home, it is often a good idea to pay off the mortgage, if possible; they do not want to expend their income on monthly debt. They may even want to take out a reverse mortgage (see Chapter 2 for details).

In Case of Emergency

What You and Your Parents Need to Know About Healthcare

The soaring cost of medical care, including prescription drugs, long-term care, and other services, and the resulting pressure on health insurance premiums have become top-priority for all Americans. This is especially true of seniors, most of whom rely on Medicare or Medicaid for their coverage. Those who can afford the premiums should avail themselves of additional coverage through one of several Medigap plans.

The recently inaugurated prescription drug plan offered through Social Security is a new, albeit still controversial, and complicated plan, aimed at alleviating the high cost of prescription drugs. To date, only private insurance and Medicaid are available to meet the needs some seniors have for long-term care in nursing homes and other facilities as well as in-home care—all of which carry high costs. (More about these programs later in the chapter.)

The best health coverage might be through the company from which your parent retired even if they must pay the full premiums. Your parents might find a good Health Maintenance Organization (HMO) or Preferred Provider Organization (PPO) that provides good care and controls health costs. Medicare Advantage, discussed in detail below, is a new program that offers this option. If your parent's income is low enough, they can also qualify for Medicaid. If dad is a veteran, he may be able to obtain medical care through the Department of Veterans Affairs (VA).

If your parents anticipate needing a nursing home or medical care in their own residence, they should look into the many long-term-care policies offered by insurance companies. The earlier they buy such a policy, the less expensive the premiums will be. If they purchase the policy right before they need the benefits, it will be prohibitively expensive, if it is available at all.

▶ Trip Protection: Medical Insurance

Years ago, health insurance was relatively simple. You went to the doctor of your choice who billed your insurance carrier directly, or you paid the bill and submitted it for reimbursement. Now, there are many more choices. Do you want the traditional fee-for-service indemnity plan? How about opting for the Health Maintenance Organization (HMO) or Preferred Provider Organization (PPO) alternative? Despite these complexities, it is crucial that you and your parent(s) understand their health insurance options and maximize their benefits at the least possible cost. Adequate health insurance is critical because your parent(s) can easily be devastated financially if they need major surgery or long-term medical care.

Not only are most seniors required to pay part of their Medicare health insurance premiums, but, even if they have a Medigap plan, their deductibles and co-payments are costly. Future changes in health insurance coverage provided by the government are likely to cost them even more money and angst, so it's important that you and your parent(s) keep up with the changes and understand your options.

Short Trips: Medicare Coverage

For those age 65 or older, and we're assuming your parent is, Medicare provides substantial health insurance benefits—whether your parent is retired or still working.

Medicare, by the way, should not be confused with Medicaid, which is a jointly funded, federal-state health insurance program for certain low-income and needy people (more on Medicaid later in this section). Medicare is a federal program available to all U.S. citizens over age 65 except for those covered by the Railroad Retirement program, which offers comparable coverage. Some people who are under 65, such as the disabled and those requiring kidney dialysis, are also covered. People who do not have a work history or have never married may not be covered (nontraditional couples, for example, with a stay-at-home partner).

Medicare Part A covers hospital expenses. Coverage is automatic. Part B coverage is elective and requires that the recipient pay a monthly premium. Your mom or dad must apply for Part B, and can sign up at a local Social Security office, three months before or after they turn 65. It's a good idea to enroll when dad first is eligible for Medicare, which he can do at his local Social Security office or by calling Social Security at 800-772-1213.

Medicare does not cover all health care costs. It is designed to cover part of a person's expenses for short-term acute medical problems rather than long-term conditions requiring custodial care. It pays for hospitalization, surgery, doctor bills, and a *very* limited amount of home health care, and skilled nursing care considered to be medically necessary and *within reasonable cost limits.*

As mentioned, the original Medicare program consists of two parts: Medicare Part A helps cover inpatient care in hospitals, skilled nursing facilities, home health, and hospice care if certain conditions are met. It's a pay-per-visit arrangement and generally does not cover outpatient prescriptions, dental services, hearing aids, most eyeglasses, or long-term nursing care.

If your mom is eligible, she can enroll without charge; however, if she is not covered by Social Security, she must pay part of the premium (see below for information on premium costs, co-insurance, and deductibles). When mom applies for Social Security benefits, she automatically applies for Medicare. If mom plans to work past age 65, she should still apply for Medicare. Following are the expenses that Medicare Part A covers:

1. Hospitalization. After mom meets her deductible, Medicare pays all costs from her first through 60th day in the hospital. From her 61st through 90th day, Medicare covers her full costs after she meets her coinsurance payments, meaning the portion of the daily cost of hospitalization that she must pay out-of-pocket.

2. Nursing-home care. Medicare pays 100 percent of *approved* amounts for her first 20 days of care in a skilled-nursing facility *after* she has been in the hospital for at least three days. This means she can't go from home to nursing home; there must be at least three consecutive days spent in a hospital.

3. Home health care. Medicare pays 100 percent of any approved home health care services, as well as 80 percent of approved medical equipment.

4. Hospice care. Medicare covers all costs, though it sets limits for outpatient drugs and inpatient respite care.

The second part of the original Medicare program is Part B, which is optional. It is meant to help cover the cost of doctors' services (but not routine physical exams), outpatient medical and surgical services and supplies, diagnostic tests, ambulatory surgery center facility fees for approved procedures, ambulance, outpatient therapy, and other professional services. It also covers durable medical equipment like wheelchairs, hospital beds, oxygen, and walkers when they are medically necessary, as defined by Medicare. Part B also includes some other medical services not listed in Part A coverage.

Your parent should sign up for Part B because it covers:

1. Medical services. After dad meets his deductible, Part B pays 80 percent of approved amounts for doctors, surgeons, supplies, and medical equipment (wheelchair) and supplies (oxygen); outpatient surgery; physical and occupational therapy; ambulance services; some limited psychiatry, podiatry, and chiropractic care; and second opinions.

2. Tests. Part B pays 100 percent of approved amounts for medical tests, laboratory work, biopsies, X-rays, and blood work, including annual mammograms, Pap tests, colonoscopy, bone density tests, PSA tests, and glaucoma screening. It also pays 100 percent of approved amounts for flu and pneumonia shots, diabetic supplies and education and nutrition therapy, and kidney failure treatments.

3. Home health care. Part B pays for all costs of approved home health care services, with no deductible. In addition, it covers 80 percent of the cost of medical equipment used in the home, after a deductible.

4. Outpatient hospital care. Part B covers 80 percent of any approved procedures performed in a hospital on an outpatient basis.

5. Blood. The plan pays for 80 percent of the cost of approved amounts of blood after the first three pints.

While the list of services that Medicare covers seems extensive, many medical expenses are excluded. For example, Medicare does not reimburse for:

▶ Nursing care beyond 100 days in a skilled-nursing facility; private nursing care; and any care in a center not approved by Medicare

▶ Custodial and intermediate nursing care

▶ Prescription drugs not given in a hospital

▶ Routine physicals, dentistry, acupuncture, immunizations, cosmetic surgery, and foot, eye, and hearing care

▶ Doctor charges that exceed approved Medicare levels or that Medicare does not consider medically necessary. Each year, the government publishes a fee schedule listing maximum Medicare payments, which are usually far less than doctors charge regular commercial patients.

▶ Care in foreign countries, except in certain limited circumstances in Canada and Mexico

Because Medicare coverage is limited in so many ways, several plans have been designed to fill in the gaps. These plans are called Medigap policies and are discussed in more detail in the next section.

Medicare Costs. Medicare is not free and requires cost sharing in the form of premiums, deductibles, and coinsurance. Generally, people who have worked for 40 quarters or 10 full years are eligible for premium-free Medicare Part A. However, deductibles do apply. Those who have worked less than 40 quarters must pay a premium as well as deductibles. As of January 2005, the Part A premium is $206.00 for people having 30 to 39 quarters of Medicare-covered employment and $375.00 per month for people who are not otherwise eligible for premium-free hospital insurance and have less than 30 quarters of Medicare-covered employment.

The following deductibles apply (as of January 2005) for each benefit period (meaning, hospital stay), your parent pays:

▶ A total of $912 for a hospital stay of one to 60 days.

▶ $228 per day for days 61 to 90 of a hospital stay.

▶ $456 per day for days 91 to 150 of a hospital stay (Lifetime Reserve Days).

▶ All costs for each day beyond 150 days.

▶ $114 per day for days 21 through 100 of each benefit period for skilled nursing facility care (Part A pays 100 percent for the first 20 days.)

Effective January 2005, the monthly premium for Medicare Part B is $78.20 per month, which is deducted automatically from Social Security checks. In addition to the premium, there's a Medicare Part B annual deductible ($110 in 2005). Your parent then pays 20 percent of the Medicare-approved amount for services after the deductible is met. Premium amounts likely will change every January.

Medicare Advantage. Medicare advantage (formerly called Medicare + Choice) is an alternative to the original Medicare. Your parent must be enrolled in Medicare Part A and Part B to join a Medicare Advantage Plan. These plans are Health Maintenance Organizations (HMOs), where dad can choose doctors from among those in that organization, or modified HMOs known as Preferred Provider Organizations (PPOs). A PPO provides an HMO facility but allows members to go to providers outside the network for Medicare-covered services. The PPO option usually costs more than the self-contained HMO option. Everything covered in the original Medicare Parts A and B is offered by the Medicare Advantage options. In addition, dad may be able to get extra benefits like coverage for prescription drugs and more preventive and wellness services. The plans vary depending upon where a person lives; you or dad can easily check his options by visiting http://www.medicare.gov. What follows is a general description of what he can expect to receive from an HMO and a PPO. Note: The original Medicare is a private, fee-for-service option that allows dad to go to any doctor or hospital. Services will be reimbursed according to the schedules listed above. Additional costs may be supplemented by various Medigap plans, which we will explore in the next section.

The HMO (Health Maintenance Organization) Alternative. Instead of choosing one's own doctors and getting reimbursed for expenses under the traditional fee-for-service health insurance plan, when dad becomes an HMO member, he has unlimited access to the organization's medical services. He can visit a doctor for preventive checkups, minor problems, or emergencies.

If the HMO runs a central medical facility, he must go there for all procedures.

However, if he is out of town, the HMO will reimburse him for visits to approved doctors or hospitals. In a true life-or-death emergency, he can go to any hospital and still get reimbursed.

Roadmap 4.1

Medicare Myths and Misconceptions

1. *Doctors welcome new Medicare patients.* Some do, but others limit their number of Medicare patients. As reimbursement for services drops, so does the number of doctors willing to serve the senior population. Typically, doctors will continue to see a patient who turns 65 while under their care. However, if your mom moves or seeks a new physician, she may be unable to find a practice that will accept her unless she also has private insurance.

2. *Medicare will cover my nursing home needs.* It will cover the first 20 days of care in full; then dad must pay $114 per day for days 21 through 100; after which he must cover all costs for any benefit period. He must be improving rapidly and significantly, and he must need skilled nursing care. Custodial care in a nursing home or assisted living facility is not covered.

3. *I can give my assets away, let the government pay the bills, and guarantee my family's inheritance.* The misconception persists that, by artificially impoverishing yourself, your care will be covered by government subsidy via Medicaid, a program for the medically indigent of any age. Aside from the questionable ethics of organizing mom's affairs in this manner, there are some very real arguments against this.

   There is a look-back period of three years for direct gifting and five years for assets conveyed to trusts. Also, some states aggressively pursue recapture of estate assets when a Medicaid recipient dies. If her motivation is to provide for her heirs, she may have her last wishes denied. If she has resources, she may be better served by purchasing long-term care coverage rather than relying on this government program.

For more details on the expenses Medicare covers, as well as the current cost of deductibles, co-payments, and premiums, call the Social Security Administration's Medicare hotline at 800-772-1213, or obtain a copy of the *Medicare Handbook* from any Social Security office, or visit http://www.medicare.gov or http://www.senioranswers.org.

An HMO offers several advantages:

1. Dad's total out-of-pocket costs are limited.
2. He does not have to deal with deductibles, co-payments, or coverage limits.
3. He will not have to search for a generalist or specialist practitioner because the HMO employs every type of physician he will probably ever need. However, if he has an extremely rare condition that no one on the HMO's staff can handle, the HMO will locate a specialist.
4. All of his medical records are kept in one place, so that his medical history is immediately available to whatever doctor treats him.

The downside of HMOs is that what dad gains in financial control he loses in medical choice.

1. He cannot bring his existing doctor to the HMO, so he must choose a new primary care physician from a list provided by the HMO.
2. If his chosen doctor is not available on the day he visits the clinic, he must see whoever is working.
3. If he needs a specialist, he must select one from the HMO's approved list, regardless of whether the doctor is the best person in town. In addition, many HMO generalists hate to refer patients to specialists because it costs the HMO more, and one of the main goals of HMOs is to control costs.

The same lack of choice applies to hospitals: Dad must go where the HMO sends him, which may not be the hospital he'd prefer. If he seeks help at a hospital not specifically authorized by his HMO, he will probably have to pay the entire bill on his own.

Before dad decides to join an HMO, ask plenty of questions. Following are a few areas to explore:

1. Do either you or your dad know anyone on the plan, and, if so, what has that person's experience been?
2. How competent are the doctors? What percentage are board-certified? (The more doctors who are board-certified, meaning they successfully passed a specialty test, the better. The average certification rate is about 70 percent.)
3. How long do patients wait for an appointment to see a specialist?

4. Is preventive medicine encouraged or discouraged? If encouraged, specifically what does the HMO do to minimize medical problems?
5. How are HMO members treated at HMO-affiliated hospitals?
6. Is the HMO accredited? (This is not required, but it is certainly better to join an accredited HMO than an unaccredited one. Agencies such as the National Committee for Quality Assurance set the most stringent standards.)
7. Is there a high staff turnover rate at the HMO he is interested in? (A high rate can mean that the patient load is too large and that doctors are unhappy.)
8. What is the member retention rate? (A higher rate indicates a better level of member satisfaction. Good HMOs conduct annual patient surveys. Review them to gain insight into member satisfaction.)

For an evaluation of a managed care plan dad is thinking of using, contact the National Committee for Quality Assurance by calling 888-275-7585 or go to their Web site, http://www.ncqa.org. NCQA is a private, not-for-profit organization dedicated to assessing and reporting on the quality of managed care plans.

The PPO (Preferred Provider Organization) Alternative. Somewhere between the traditional fee-for-service plan and the HMO is the PPO, which enlists the services of generalist and specialist doctors, hospitals, and many other health care providers. These caregivers receive a set monthly fee to provide a set level of services. If they give more care than was agreed on, they earn more money.

From mom's point of view, her costs will probably be lower under a PPO than a traditional plan because the medical professionals and hospitals in the network offer discounts in exchange for a steady flow of patients. However, PPOs give her more choice over which doctor she may see because she can go to anyone who is part of the network. If she visits a doctor who does not work for the PPO, she will be reimbursed by the health insurance company at a reduced rate. For example, she might get back 70 percent of the bill instead of 80 percent. When investigating a PPO, ask questions similar to those posed for HMOs.

Uncharted Waters: Medicare Prescription Drug Benefit

As we all know, the cost of paying for prescription drugs has been increasing every year, especially for seniors. Medicare pays for some prescriptions, for example, certain cancer drugs, but Medicare doesn't cover everything. Many people with Medicare have prescription drug coverage through other insurance like an employer group health plan, a Medicare Managed Care plan, or a Medigap policy. Even with this coverage, your dad may still have trouble paying for his prescriptions.

Beginning January 1, 2006, new Medicare prescription drug plans will be available to people with Medicare. Insurance companies and other private companies will work with Medicare to offer these drug plans. They will negotiate discounts on drug prices. These plans are different from the Medicare-approved drug discount cards, which phase out by May 15, 2006, or when your enrollment in a Medicare prescription drug plan takes effect, if earlier.

Medicare prescription drug plans provide insurance coverage for prescription drugs. Like other insurance, if dad joins he will pay a monthly premium (generally around $37 in 2006) and a share of the cost of his prescriptions. Costs will vary depending on the drug plan he chooses. In addition, drug plans may vary in what prescription drugs are covered, how much beneficiaries have to pay, and which pharmacies can be used. All drug plans will have to provide at least a standard level of coverage, which Medicare will set. However, some plans might offer more coverage and additional drugs for a higher monthly premium. When dad joins a drug plan, it is important for him to choose one that meets his prescription drug needs.

As we go to press, the details of the various plans are not available; however, we do know the basics. Coverage for the drug benefit will be provided by private Prescription Drug Plans (PDPs) that offer drug-only coverage, or through Medicare Advantage plans that offer both prescription drug and health care coverage (known as MA-PD plans). All of these plans are referred to as Part D plans. These plans must offer a standard drug benefit, but will have the flexibility to vary the drug benefit within certain parameters.

Assistance with premiums and cost sharing will be provided to eligible low-income beneficiaries. Part D covers many, but not all, of the drugs that are approved under the Medicaid program, provided they are dispensed by prescription and on an outpatient basis for a medically accepted reason (although selection may be restricted).

Although drug plan sponsors may change some of the specifications, the benefit offered must at least be equal in value to the standard benefit. In 2006, standard coverage includes:

1. A monthly premium estimated on average to be about $37 (a beneficiary may pay a higher or lower amount depending upon which PDP or MA-PD the beneficiary selects).
2. A deductible of $250.
3. Coinsurance of 25 percent (or cost-sharing on average equal to coinsurance of 25 percent) up to an initial coverage limit of $2,250.
4. Protection against high out-of-pocket prescription drug costs, with co-pays generally of the greater of $2 for generic drugs and preferred multiple source drugs and $5 for all other drugs or 5 percent of the price, once an enrollee's out-of-pocket spending reaches a limit of $3,600.

Drugs and biological products that are paid by Medicare Part A or Part B are excluded.

Low-Income Benefit. Those beneficiaries with limited savings and low incomes will receive more generous benefit packages.

Beneficiaries with limited savings and incomes below 135 percent of the federal poverty line (which in 2004 was $12,569 for individuals, $16,862 for couples) will receive:

- ▶ A $0 deductible
- ▶ A $0 premium
- ▶ Continuation of coverage beyond the initial coverage limit
- ▶ Co-pays of $2 for generics and preferred multiple source drugs and $5 for all other drugs, up to the out-of-pocket limit.
- ▶ $0 co-pay for all prescriptions once the out-of-pocket limit is reached. The government subsidy for cost-sharing counts toward the out-of-pocket limit.

Beneficiaries with limited savings and incomes below 150 percent of the federal poverty level (which in 2004 was $13,965 for individuals; $18,735 for couples) will receive:

- ▶ A sliding scale monthly premium that will average about $18 for beneficiaries with incomes between 135 percent and 150 percent below the federal poverty level.
- ▶ A $50 deductible
- ▶ Continuation of coverage beyond the initial coverage limit
- ▶ Coinsurance of 15 percent up to the out-of-pocket limit. (The government subsidy for cost-sharing counts toward the out-of-pocket limit.)
- ▶ Co-pays of $2 for generic drugs and preferred drugs that are multiple source drugs or $5 once the out-of-pocket limit is reached.

If your dad is eligible for a full low-income premium subsidy, he will not have to pay any premium if he enrolls (or is auto-enrolled) in a plan with a monthly premium at or below the low-income premium subsidy amount.

If dad is eligible for full benefits under Medicare and Medicaid ("full-benefit dual eligible individuals") with income under 100 percent of the federal poverty line, and limited savings, the co-payment is reduced to $1 and $3, and if he is full-benefit dual eligible and living in a nursing home, there is no co-pay.

Eligibility, Election, and Enrollment. The initial enrollment period when a beneficiary first becomes eligible for Part D is similar to the initial enrollment period established for Part B. Eligibility and enrollment changed in 2005–2006. Generally, the annual election period is from November 15 to December 31 of each year.

When Travel Insurance Is Not Enough: Medigap Coverage

Because Medicare, like Social Security, is not meant to cover all costs, your dad also needs to purchase Medicare coinsurance, called Medigap or Medicare supplemental insurance (MedSup), coverage to pay for additional benefits needed as well as the 20 percent that Part B does not cover. Your dad can purchase this additional insurance through various insurance companies.

Keep in mind that 20 percent of outpatient surgery, diagnostic tests, and treatments can be costly. In addition, some supplemental policies also pay for products and services not covered by Medicare, such as outpatient prescription drugs.

Medigap policies only work with the original Medicare plan, and are available through private insurance agents. A policy can be purchased on

Tollbooth 4.1

Ask Your Doctors the Magic Medicare Question

The magic question to ask mom's health care provider is, "Do you take assignment?" If the answer is yes, that can minimize her costs. Medicare pays 80 percent of the usual and customary fee, as *determined by Medicare*. Medicare billing is capped at 115 percent of the doctor's figures. Coinsurance will pay the remaining 20 percent of the approved charges.

For example: The bill is $115. Medicare approves $100 and pays the approved 80 percent. Mom's coinsurance pays the additional 20 percent of this approved amount. Mom owes the balance up to the $115 total, which is $15. If the bill were $150, she would owe nothing above the $115, because that represents the 115 percent Medicare billing cap. However, if your mother's doctor takes assignment, she would owe nothing beyond the Medicare and coinsurance payments paid by her insurance coverage.

---

the first day of the month in which an individual turns 65 and is enrolled in Medicare Part B. There is a six-month window known as the open enrollment period. During that six-month period following dad's 65th birthday, no insurance company can deny him coverage or place conditions on his coverage because of health problems.

Currently, 10 standard Medicare supplement policies exist. They are labeled letter A through letter J for easy comparison. Policy A is the most basic and is available to all Medicare recipients. Policies B through J offer more and more benefits, and more and more people are excluded from qualification. All 10 Medigap policies cover at least the daily coinsurance amount for hospitalization under Medicare Part A. The more inclusive policies pay additional benefits for such services as preventive medical care, coverage in a foreign country, hospice care, prescription drugs, or home visits—all of which Medicare does not cover.

What plan your dad should choose depends on his anticipated lifestyle and personal economics. Does he plan to travel? Some plans will cover him outside the United States. Other plans may limit prescription benefits. Cost is the primary consideration. Keep in mind that what dad can afford now is only one part of the decision. The costs will increase with dad's age and inflation and may change if he relocates to another state. For example, the total premiums paid for Plan J (the most comprehensive and expensive plan) from ages 65 to 80 may require approximately $47,000, and $66,000 to age 85. Costs in a more expensive part of the country can run almost twice that amount. (This assumes an annual medical inflation rate of 7 percent.) See Roadmap 4.2, provided courtesy of the National Association of Insurance Commissioners (NAIC).

When shopping for a Medigap policy, make certain you and dad watch for pre-existing conditions clauses that preclude him from receiving benefits if he already has developed an ailment. Also, make sure that his policy is guaranteed renewable, and determine whether his premiums will rise with age. Finally, examine the elimination periods imposed for hospital stays. Some policies stipulate that a person has to be hospitalized several days before benefits kick in, which may mean that dad never collects a dime.

Hazard!
Caveat Emptor—Know Before You Go

The process of choosing a Medigap policy can be quite complex and confusing. Many people are pressured into making quick decisions by commission-hungry salespeople. Instead, make sure you and your dad take your time, so that you and he understand exactly what he is buying. Don't make a common mistake and purchase too much insurance; one comprehensive Medigap plan is all that he needs. According to federal law, even after a person buys a policy, he has 30 days to review it and obtain a full refund of all premiums paid.

Extended Travel: Long-Term Care Policies

Such policies cover the health costs of long-term custodial care either in a nursing home or at home. While the coverage from long-term care policies can offset some of the costs of such care, they rarely pay all the bills.

According to *The MetLife Market Survey of Nursing Home and Home Care Costs,* which was done in 2003, the national average cost per year for a private room is just under $70,000; for a semiprivate room, the cost is just short of $60,000, and home health aides average about $18 an hour (which can add up quickly, especially if mom requires round-the-clock care). Long-term care policies pay between $40 and $100 a day for nursing homes and half

Benefits Offered by Medicare Supplemental Policies

A	B	C	D	E	F	G	H	I	J
Basic benefits	Basic benefits	Basic benefits	Basic benefits	Basic benefits	Basic benefits	Basic benefits	Basic benefits	Basic benefits	Basic benefits
		Skilled nursing co-insurance	Skilled nursing co-insurance	Skilled nursing co-insurance	Skilled nursing co-insurance	Skilled nursing co-insurance	Skilled nursing co-insurance	Skilled nursing co-insurance	Skilled nursing co-insurance
	Part A deductible	Part A deductible	Part A deductible	Part A deductible	Part A deductible	Part A deductible	Part A deductible	Part A deductible	Part A deductible
		Part B deductible			Part B deductible				Part B deductible
					Part B excess (100%)	Part B excess (80%)		Part B excess (80%)	Part B excess (80%)
		Foreign travel emergency	Foreign travel emergency	Foreign travel emergency	Foreign travel emergency	Foreign travel emergency	Foreign travel emergency	Foreign travel emergency	Foreign travel emergency
			At-home recovery			At-home recovery		At-home recovery	At-home recovery
							Basic drugs ($1,250 limit)	Basic drugs ($1,250 limit)	Extended drug benefit ($3,000 limit)
				Preventative care					Preventative care

Source: Used by permission of the National Association of Insurance Commissioners.

that amount for at-home care. While some policies offer inflation-adjustment clauses, these policies should be seen as a supplement to, not a replacement for, more comprehensive policies. For a more detailed look at the best long-term care solutions, obtain a copy of the booklet *Retiree What You Need To Know About Long Term Care Guide* from the United Seniors Health Cooperative. Request a copy at their Web site at http://www.ushc-online.org.

How to Evaluate Long-term Care Policies. Understanding long-term care insurance can be a challenge because each company and policy has its own features and benefits. Some questions you and dad should be asking yourselves follow:

What Is Long-Term Care Insurance, and Why Does Dad Need It? Long-term care insurance is designed to cover the costs of caring for individuals with one or more chronic health conditions from which they are generally not expected to recover. It is not traditional medical insurance; rather, it covers skilled, intermediate, and custodial types of care, which focus primarily on assistance with activities of daily living or supervision related to cognitive impairment.

To qualify for benefits in most states, he must require substantial assistance with two of the six activities of daily living or need substantial supervision due to cognitive impairment. Depending on the state, current care costs can range from $30,000 to $100,000 a year and up. If your dad is 65 years old today, by the time he is 85, the costs will be closer to $100,000 to $550,000, due to inflation. People who save to pay for this care will pay for it with after-tax dollars. Medicaid may be an option, but it's only available if your parent meets very strict requirements.

Long-term care insurance benefits paid by tax-qualified policies that meet government specifications are free from income tax. Also, premiums paid on a tax-qualified policy may be partially deductible as a medical expense under itemized deductions on dad's income tax return. These deductions would be available to you if you were paying for your parent's insurance.

Are There Reasons Not to Purchase Long-Term Care Insurance? Yes. Don't purchase long-term care insurance if dad

- ▶ truly cannot afford the premium
- ▶ could not afford a premium increase of 10 to 20 percent
- ▶ has limited assets

▶ has only Social Security or Supplemental Security Income as an income source

▶ has trouble paying for utilities, rent, food, medicine, or other important needs

▶ can afford and prefers to pay for long-term care costs on his own.

For more information on long-term care for those who can't afford private insurance, see the section on Medicaid below.

Why Should Dad Purchase Long-Term Care Insurance? He should buy long-term care insurance if he wants to maintain his independence, retain more control over his (and your) care choices and the quality of care, or preserve as much as possible of his income and assets.

Decisions Associated with Buying Long-Term Care Insurance. You should have answers to the following questions before dad decides to purchase long-term care insurance.

1. Where does he want his care to take place? Most policies provide for care in a nursing home, an assisted-living facility, an Alzheimer's facility, an adult day care center, or in one's own home.

2. For how long does dad want to receive benefits? Options most often include two, three, four, five, six, seven, or 10 years or a lifetime. Make sure the benefit period is not split between facility care and home health care, unless dad is insured for lifetime.

3. How much money does he want as a daily benefit? Most policies provide from $50 to $300 or more, offered in $10 increments. The daily benefit is always at 100 percent for nursing home care but can be less for assisted-living facilities and/or home health care. The majority of policies pay actual expenses up to the daily benefit amount. If a company pays the prevailing cost for like services to individuals with similar health conditions in dad's locale, the amount could be less than his actual expenses. For an additional premium, he can purchase an indemnity benefit that pays the full daily benefit amount regardless of prevailing cost.

4. How long does dad want to wait after he starts receiving care for the insurance benefits to begin? This elimination period is similar to a deductible on medical insurance. Longer waiting periods will reduce his premium.

5. What, if any, protection does he want from inflation? Because the costs associated with long-term care increase faster than the average rate of

inflation, dad should consider purchasing inflation protection. Most policies offer 5 percent simple or 5 percent compound inflation protection.

Understand the Wording: Some words to watch for include substantial assistance and substantial supervision. The more lenient definitions are standby assistance for daily living activities and presence of another individual for cognitive impairment. More restrictive definitions are hands-on assistance most of the time and verbal supervision and cuing for a majority of the time, or continual supervision. The more restrictive the definition, the harder qualifying for benefits will be.

Also, look at who determines if dad qualifies for benefits and develops his plan of care. Many policies require only that a licensed health care practitioner of dad's choosing certify that he needs assistance and will need it for longer than 90 days. A few policies require that a care advisor, employed by the insurance company or by an agency with which the insurance company has a contract, be used. Finally, as with other types of insurance, the company dad selects should have a top financial rating. It also should have been in the long-term care insurance business for at least 10 years with a good history of paying claims.

Red Light Ahead: Specialized Health Insurance Policies

In addition to the usual health insurance plans, several specialized policies are marketed aggressively.

Hospital Indemnity Plans. The most widely advertised policies are hospital indemnity plans, which pay a specified amount of cash each day that a person is hospitalized. The plans are usually advertised on television or through the mail. Such pitches announce that you can get $75 a day, for example, for only pennies in premiums. The problem is that hospitals charge an average of $750 a day, and most of the hospital's services are already covered by mom's comprehensive health insurance plan. In addition, hospital indemnity plans often limit pre-existing conditions, which may prevent dad from receiving benefits. Most plans also have elimination periods, meaning that your mother must be hospitalized a certain number of days before she collects benefits. Nowadays, most hospitals try to shorten patients' stays, so it can be very difficult to collect on these policies.

Specific Disease Policies. Also known as dread disease policies, these policies play on people's fears by covering a specific disease, most commonly cancer. These pay limited benefits if mom contracts the illness named in the policy; each policy establishes a strict definition of a specific disease. For example, health problems caused by cancer usually don't entitle a person to benefits. As with hospital indemnity coverage, a good comprehensive policy costs far less money and pays benefits more readily than a disease-specific plan. In some states, insurance regulators have prohibited the sale of cancer insurance due to the questionable sales practices they could invite that take advantage of people's fears of this disease.

▶ Fork in the Road: Planning for Medicaid

Started in 1965, Medicaid is a partnership between each state and the federal government to provide medical care to the elderly, blind, and disabled poor. Unlike Medicare, eligibility for Medicaid is based on financial need. Medicaid's primary benefit is the safety net it provides for long-term nursing care for those who cannot afford it. Currently, Medicaid covers more than half of the long-term care costs in the United States.

It's an extremely complex system that's handled differently in each state. We can only address the general basics; you and mom should check with the state to understand its unique guidelines. Applications for Medicaid coverage are made with the appropriate state agency. Substantial documentation and paperwork are required.

Eligibility Requirements. Following are the basic requirements for Medicaid eligibility:

- ▶ U.S. citizenship or qualified alien status.
- ▶ Residency in the state where the application is made.
- ▶ Medical need. You must need long-term care, usually determined by the inability to perform at least two of the activities of daily living without assistance. The six major activities are dressing; transferring, such as getting from a bed to a chair; using the bathroom; eating; bathing; and maintaining continence.
- ▶ Limited financial resources. The first of the two financial requirements, generally this means that the individual applying for Medicaid cannot have available resources or assets exceeding $2,000. If married, the

spouse cannot have more than $90,660 (in 2003) in available resources. Generally, the following count as exceptions to "available resources":

1. Home. It's excluded as long as mom intends to return there or her spouse resides there.
2. Vehicle. The maximum exempt value for an automobile varies from state to state.
3. Household goods. These generally are exempt unless they are of unusual value.
4. Property or tools. Those used in her trade or business and necessary for support.
5. Life insurance. Only policies up to $1,500 are not included. If the total face value is higher, the cash surrender value counts.
6. Burial plot. Prepaid burial expenses and an account designated for funeral arrangements are generally allowed up to $1,500.

▶ Income cap. Almost half the states have an income cap. It varies, but most states fix it at 300 percent of the current monthly maximum Supplemental Social Security benefit (in 2005, $579 per month for an individual and $869 per couple). Other states are "medically needy states," where income eligibility for Medicaid is the inability to pay the actual cost of private care from the income available.

Watch Out: Impoverishment Strategies Can Backfire. Essentially, to qualify for Medicaid, mom must exhaust all other assets except her house, car, and household belongings. In the past, Medicaid applicants from middle-income and wealthy backgrounds worked with attorneys and financial planners to figure out ways to "impoverish" themselves (usually by giving away assets to family members), then have Medicaid foot the bill for their long-term care. But Congress has passed two laws that attach criminal penalties to such actions. Despite enforceability and constitutionality issues associated with each, clearly the intent of Congress is that those who can afford their own long-term care should pay for it, not Medicaid.

For Medicaid planning purposes, Medicaid applicants cannot just give away assets to qualify for coverage. The rules include a look-back period for gifts by an applicant or spouse. Gifts given over the past three years prior to the application (five years if the transfer was made from a trust) still count as assets in determining Medicaid eligibility.

Other Pitfalls and Mistakes. Another mistake that applicants sometimes make is purchasing an annuity to reduce their assets. That only works when done properly and under certain circumstances. Care has to be taken that it is the proper type of annuity and that the income from the annuity will not cause the Medicaid applicant's income level to be too high in the state where the application is being made.

Perhaps of even greater concern is the level of care that Medicaid patients receive. Facilities often have a limited number of Medicaid beds, and some argue that Medicaid patients receive lower-quality care than private payers. That's one reason to consider long-term care insurance.

Travel Documents

Estate Planning and Other Hard-to-Discuss Topics

Though thinking about it may make you and them uncomfortable, your parents will die someday. When that unfortunate event occurs, whether it is tomorrow or decades from now, their assets will be distributed, and their estate may have to pay estate taxes. What your parents should decide now is whether they want to control how their estate is settled or leave it up to the probate court, which might distribute their property in a manner that would not please them if they were alive.

We hope that as you read this chapter, both parents are alive, and, for the most part, what we write in this chapter assumes that that is the case. That's because estate planning is an ongoing process; something both parents should plan for before either becomes ill and which should continue for the remainder of each of their lives. How they plan will affect the lives of the widow(er) and may, if you become responsible for the care of one or both parents, affect your life as well.

When your parents, and perhaps even you, hear the word estate, they may envision something big and grandiose and far beyond their own financial reality—a mansion, for example. However, in the eyes of the law, their estate is simply everything they own, by themselves or with others. Their home, car, furniture, bank accounts, jewelry, life insurance policy, retirement plan, stocks and bonds, and other assets are all part of their estate. Although some people have large estates worth millions, the estates of most Americans are relatively modest.

Regardless of the size of your parents' estate, if they ignore the process of estate planning, they not only lose control of how their worldly possessions will be handed out, but their estate might pay thousands of dollars in estate taxes that could easily have been avoided.

On the other hand, if they make the effort to maximize basic estate planning techniques, their spouse, children, grandchildren, and others for whom they care deeply will receive a far greater inheritance to enrich their lives. If your parents never made an estate plan and are reluctant or simply fearful of going forward with one, explain to them that though the will might not benefit them personally, it would ensure that the fruits of their life's labor is passed onto their loved ones the way they wanted it. Perhaps, even more important, explain that estate planning involves more than money; that the creation of a living will and other healthcare directives can have a very direct effect upon how they will be treated in the event they become ill or incapacitated. Explain, too, that if they choose, they can have a say in their funeral plans.

As we've said, estate planning and related subjects, like living wills and healthcare directives, are often difficult subjects to broach to a parent. You may feel awkward discussing these issues with your parents; similarly your parents may not want to involve you directly in their decision-making or may want only to involve you in certain aspects of it. Regardless of how they do it—in consultation with you and other family members or with legal, financial, and health professionals—it is vital that they do it. As their situations change, make sure that the plan is appropriately reviewed and modified, if necessary.

▶ Getting Through Customs: Estate Planning

While this chapter will not cover the details of estate planning, it will provide an overview of what should be considered as your parents plan their estates.

Estate planning is a process, not a product. It involves seeking advice, reviewing options, and creating a plan for ensuring that your parents'

- ▶ assets are sufficient to meet their objectives for their heirs;
- ▶ heirs receive those assets in the proportion, manner, and timeframe your parents choose;
- ▶ income taxes, estate taxes, gift taxes, inheritance taxes, and transfer costs are minimized and then paid as cheaply as possible; and
- ▶ that liquidity exists to pay taxes and transfer costs when they are due.

Getting Directions: What Estate Planning Entails

Because the term estate planning is mysterious to many people, the following list provides a quick look at some of the key areas covered by the term, and may help in your discussions with your parents:

- ▶ Choosing who gets how much of their money and possessions that remain after the costs of settling the estate are subtracted.
- ▶ Preparing a strategy to give away many of their assets as tax-free gifts while they live to minimize the assets socked by estate taxes when they die.
- ▶ Selecting a trustee to administer any trusts they may establish.
- ▶ Nominating an executor of their estate, who should be an independent person they trust, to carry out the provisions of their will faithfully. Often, this is a lawyer familiar with the family.
- ▶ Deciding what should be done with their bodies after they die. They may want it donated for medical research or cremated, for instance. Also, specifying how and where they want to be buried. Some people even limit what they want spent on their funerals.
- ▶ Appointing a successor custodian for the assets of a child or grandchild if they currently act as a custodian for a Uniform Gifts to Minors Act account. If they don't specify the successor custodian, a court will decide for them.
- ▶ Planning to make gifts of either money or property to their favorite charity, university, church, or synagogue. Without specific written instructions, no such gifts can be authorized by the executor of their estate.
- ▶ Preparing for the time they are unable to care for themselves. They can prepare what are called advance directives giving instructions on what kinds of health care they want provided or withheld in the event they cannot communicate their wishes. (More on living wills and other advance directives in the next section.)

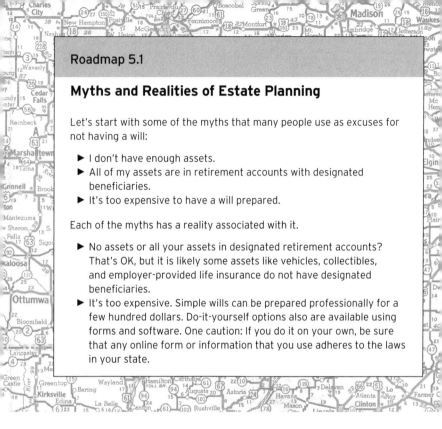

Roadmap 5.1

Myths and Realities of Estate Planning

Let's start with some of the myths that many people use as excuses for not having a will:

- ► I don't have enough assets.
- ► All of my assets are in retirement accounts with designated beneficiaries.
- ► It's too expensive to have a will prepared.

Each of the myths has a reality associated with it.

- ► No assets or all your assets in designated retirement accounts? That's OK, but it is likely some assets like vehicles, collectibles, and employer-provided life insurance do not have designated beneficiaries.
- ► It's too expensive. Simple wills can be prepared professionally for a few hundred dollars. Do-it-yourself options also are available using forms and software. One caution: If you do it on your own, be sure that any online form or information that you use adheres to the laws in your state.

Clearly, it is far better to determine how they want their estate handled long before the inevitable day comes when such decisions must be made.

Though the process of estate planning usually involves several professionals, such as lawyers, financial planners, insurance agents, and accountants, it does not have to be so involved. Several do-it-yourself books on the market can help them draw up a simple will and prepare other documents that will be useful in various life situations. If you own a computer, several easy-to-use computer programs ask a series of questions, and then format the answers into legal documents that will protect your parents and their estate against almost every eventuality. They can also obtain a standard will that they can customize to meet their circumstances from a legal clinic or local law firm.

Legal books, software, and clinics will take care of most common situations and are adequate if your parents have few assets and a limited number of people to whom they want those assets distributed. However, if they hold substantial assets, or their wishes for giving away assets are complicated, they should think about assembling a team of financial experts to make sure that their will covers every contingency. And because estate and probate laws vary from state to state, it is important to have their wills drawn in accordance with local laws by an attorney familiar with them.

Mapping the Plan: The Basics of Writing and Executing a Will

Whether they do it themselves or with the help of legal advisors, writing a will is key to estate planning. A will is, quite simply, a legal declaration that gives instructions on how to dispose of assets when the person dies. Your parents can divide their assets any way they want, as long as guidelines are presented clearly in writing. (Some states prohibit clauses in wills that are considered illegal, bizarre, or against public policy.)

The portion of their estate covered by the will includes both tangible assets, like homes, cars, boats, artwork, collectibles, and furniture, as well as intangible assets, like bank accounts, stocks, bonds, and mutual funds. To specify that certain people should inherit particular tangible assets, they should include a provision known as a Tangible Personal Property Memorandum (TPPM).

Other rights and benefits, like pension rights and life insurance proceeds, are normally handled outside of a will. For example, life insurance proceeds are usually payable directly to beneficiaries. And property owned jointly with right of survivorship, such as a home owned by both parents, is not affected by the will because, by law, it passes to that joint owner automatically when one of them dies. Also, any property that they have placed in a trust passes to the beneficiary without going through their will or probate. Because trusts take assets out of their probate estate, they can save their estate a lot of money.

Most people create what is known as a simple will, which provides for the outright distribution of assets to beneficiaries. If your parents' will establishes trusts to receive assets, it is a testamentary trust will. If they set up trusts before their deaths and the will passes assets into those trusts, it is a pour-over will.

Husbands and wives can write their wills either jointly or separately. Most estate lawyers suggest separate wills because it is difficult to establish who owns which property in a joint will. In addition, after one spouse dies, it is troublesome for the surviving spouse to change the provisions in a joint will. And if they are not careful, a joint will might deprive them of the full lifetime tax-exempt inheritance that both husband and wife are allowed to pass on to heirs free of federal estate tax.

Another important aspect of a will is choosing an executor of their estate. This can be either a long-time, trusted friend or family member with knowledge of financial affairs or an institution, like a bank or law firm, with financial and legal expertise. The executor's task is to carry out your parents' wishes as set forth in the will as efficiently as possible. This process may take several months, or it may drag on for years. If they trust the executor completely, they should give the executor enough authority to take action so that the executor does not have to buy a surety bond (sometimes called a fidelity bond), which insures your estate against malfeasance by the executor. The cost of that bond, which can be substantial, is paid by your estate.

Alternate Route: Revocable Living Trusts

A document that functions much like a will is a Revocable Living Trust (Inter Vivos Trust). The benefits of living trusts are often exaggerated while the costs of establishing them (often $1,500 per and up) are understated. For example, living trusts offer no tax advantages not provided by a well-written will. If your parents have never done estate planning or haven't done it in some time, they should understand that they each now have a lifetime exemption of $2 million in assets (in 2006) that they can pass on to their heirs tax free, either through a will or through a living trust.

If your parents choose to go this route, they contribute some, or all, of their assets to the trust while they are alive. Because it's revocable, they may change its provisions or even revoke the trust anytime, for any reason, during their lifetimes. The two main benefits of revocable living trusts are the avoidance of the probate process and costs and to provide instructions to others during a period of incapacity (as opposed to only after death, as with a will). While it is a very useful estate tool, it is not for everyone.

Your parents should not set up a revocable living trust until they understand its pros and cons. The advantages of a living trust are

1. They can be both trustee and beneficiary of a living trust, which means they can control, as well as benefit from, the trust assets while living.

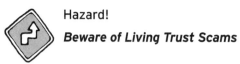

Hazard!

Beware of Living Trust Scams

It's time for a note of caution about living trusts. Fraud may also occur. Salespersons are in the business of convincing people that they need a living trust and that they can substitute one for a will. Often they use misinformation and scare tactics to make their sale. A typical sales pitch warns consumers that probate will eat up their hard-earned assets and that it could be years before their beneficiaries would ever receive what they leave them in their wills. This message may be conveyed through a living trust seminar, direct mail, newspaper ads, and even door-to-door sales. Consult with a reputable estate planning attorney.

2. The trust provides direction if they are medically or physically unable to manage their own financial affairs while living.

3. It gives them maximum flexibility and control regarding when and under what conditions their beneficiary(s) can receive the trust assets.

4. They have more control over specifically how assets will transfer to heirs.

5. Estate assets are more immediately accessible to their heirs, because they are not tied up in the probate process.

6. It is harder for disgruntled heirs to challenge a living trust compared to challenging a will.

7. Because it eliminates probate, which is a public record, it maintains privacy as to the ultimate disposition of their assets.

8. Real estate titles held in another state are more easily transferred.

Its disadvantages include:

1. They still need to execute a will, although they will probably need a much simpler will.

2. A living trust is a relatively expensive estate planning tool compared with other tools.

3. A living trust does not protect their estate from creditors.

4. It provides no additional income or estate tax advantages, although it can be combined with other kinds of trusts to save on estate taxes.

Given the time and expense involved in setting up a living trust, your parents should not establish one until they have weighed its benefits versus its costs and then compared them to the costs and benefits of other estate planning tools available to them. When you make this analysis and comparison, they should keep their estate planning goals in mind. They may conclude that there are easier and less expensive ways to achieve those goals. They should also keep in mind that most states offer modestly sized estates a cheaper and faster alternative to the formal probate process. If their estate qualifies for this alternative, there may be no need for them to incur the costs of setting up a living trust.

Passport: Financial Power of Attorney

Financial power of attorney, or durable power of attorney for finance, provides for the appointment of a person(s) to make financial decisions for each of your parents. This power may go into effect immediately on signing the document, or it may be delayed until an event occurs that triggers the power or until your parent is unable to manage their own financial affairs.

This type of planning is especially important if you are a business owner and your family depends on the business for its livelihood. Without such planning, your business could be financially damaged or ruined and your family's finances devastated.

The power of attorney can include specific provisions allowing for financial activities that may otherwise cease if your parent becomes incapacitated. It can also be set up to apply to a specific transaction. Regardless of what

Hazard!
Put It In Writing

Before your parents give someone a power of attorney for their personal or business affairs, they should check with their bank to make sure that the power of attorney document allows immediate access to the funds they have at that bank. If not, they will need to prepare whatever other documentation the bank requires to have that access. It is also a good idea to get the bank's written approval of your power of attorney after you've prepared it. That way you can be sure that there will be no glitches if their power of attorney has to be activated.

kind of power of attorney your parents give someone, they must do it while they are mentally competent and understand their actions.

If their estate is modest and they want to make sure that their personal or business affairs will be well managed if they become incapacitated, a durable power of attorney can be an inexpensive alternative to establishing a trust and naming a trustee to manage their affairs. In fact, a durable power of attorney is sometimes called a poor man's trust.

If they don't give someone a durable power of attorney and they become unable to manage their own affairs, your family can ask the court to appoint a guardian for them. However, the court process can be expensive and emotionally difficult. It can also take time, leaving your parents' affairs in limbo until a guardian is appointed. Also, the person the court appoints as your guardian may not be someone your parents would want making decisions for them if they could speak for themselves.

As with all financial and legal decisions, it is important that your parents carefully consider to whom they give this power. Once in force, the individual with the power of attorney will be able to represent your parents in any financial affairs at any time. Your parents should consult with an attorney for rules that may be specific to their state of residence or domicile.

Note: Your parents need not give the power of attorney of finance to the same person—dad and mom could give it two different persons. Also, remember the person who gets the financial power of attorney need not be the same person who gets the power of attorney for health care (see below).

Future Travel: Changing Plans for Changing Times

Estate planning is not a one-shot deal. Ideally your parents have reviewed and updated their estate plan at many different stages throughout their lives. As they age, they must continue this practice; or if they haven't been doing it regularly, they should begin to do so. Their plan will be affected by changes in their family, their wealth, their health, their charitable interests, and the laws and regulations that govern wealth transfer and taxation.

The consequences of not planning for the transfer of their estate can be severe.

1. If they die without a will, the state creates one for them. It may or may not be what they would have wanted. In some states, dying without a will results in most of their assets going to their children, with only a small remainder left for the surviving spouse.

Roadmap 5.2

Is Your Parent's Estate Plan Up-to-Date?

Your parents (and you, if you are directly involved) should review the following list periodically and discuss any shortcomings with their professional financial, tax, and legal advisers. Depending on their ages, whether or not they have already retired, some of these questions may not be applicable, but you should encourage them to review those questions that affect them periodically.

1. Do you have a written estate plan?

   ▶ Do you understand it?
   ▶ Has it been reviewed within the past three years?
   ▶ Does it include an analysis of all potential strategies?
   ▶ Did you fully implement the selected strategies?

2. Do you have a will?

   ▶ Has it been reviewed within the past three years?
   ▶ Was it updated when you moved to a new state, remarried or divorced, or experienced any other significant family change?
   ▶ Have you made appropriate provisions for any special-needs children?
   ▶ Are you comfortable with the executor(s) and trustee(s) you selected?

3. Have you considered a living trust to avoid probate?

   ▶ If you have a living trust, have you retitled your assets in the name of that trust?

4. Have you delegated appropriate powers of attorney so that, in the event of your mental or physical incompetence, your affairs can be managed by people you choose?

5. Are you taking full advantage of the marital deduction?

   ▶ Have you considered establishing a credit shelter (A/B or marital) trust?

6. Have you set up irrevocable life insurance trusts to ensure your life insurance proceeds are not taxed as part of your estate?

   ▶ Did you retitle existing life insurance policies to the trust?
   ▶ Is the amount of insurance in the trust sufficient to pay estimated taxes and transfer costs due at your death? Have you reviewed this estimate within the last three years?
   ▶ If you need to add more insurance to the trust, have you done so?
   ▶ Are you routinely sending out the required letters for any irrevocable life insurance trust?

7. Are you taking maximum advantage of the $11,000 annual gift tax exclusions?

   ▶ Have you considered annual gifts to your children and grandchildren?
   ▶ If so, do you make them outright gifts or gifts to a trust for their benefit?

8. Are you taking maximum advantage of medical and education gift tax exclusions?

   ▶ Do you have grandchildren in college (or private/parochial elementary or high schools) who could use help with their tuition?
   ▶ Do you have family members in hospitals or nursing homes who could use help with their medical bills?

9. If you have highly appreciated assets that don't generate current income, have you considered using them to fund a charitable remainder trust or other charitable gifting strategy?

10. If you are a sole proprietor, a partner, or an owner of a closely held corporation:

    ▶ Do you have a buy-sell agreement for the business?
    ▶ Have you considered key person life and disability coverage?
    ▶ Is there a written business continuation plan?

The bottom line: If your parents have taken the time to create a net worth, and/or have desires to express their wishes should they become incapacitated or upon death, they need to complete the process by careful and skillful transition planning.

2. If their estate is illiquid and they have not planned for estate tax payment, valuable assets may have to be sold quickly to pay estate taxes. This could mean having to sell the family farm or business that they wanted to give, intact, to their children. It could mean having to sell securities or real estate when the market is down. And it might even mean selling your surviving spouse's home.

3. Estate tax, inheritance tax, and transfer costs can take between 20 and 40 percent of your hard-earned estate away—before it goes to your heirs. Planning in advance can significantly increase the amount going to the people and charities you care about.

▶ Know Your Route: Honoring Your Parent's Wishes

Even if your parents have a will, that's not enough to be prepared properly. For most people, the odds of becoming medically or mentally incapacitated at any given moment are actually higher than the odds of dying. It is also possible that you may become physically or mentally incapacitated for a limited period and unable to manage your own affairs. Estate planning also includes planning for how decisions related to your personal affairs will be made under such circumstances.

For these reasons, your parents need a series of ancillary documents that address incapacity and other issues short of death. Therefore an important part of estate planning is preparing the appropriate medical documents, which generally include the following:

▶ A directive to physicians, sometimes known as a Living Will, tells medical personnel what, if any, means of artificial life support you would want and under what circumstances, in the event of your medical incapacity.

▶ A Durable Power of Attorney for Healthcare, which names someone to make medical decisions if you can't.

In this section, we'll review some of the tools they can use to control their health and medical care when they can't speak for themselves.

Visas: The Living Will and Health Care Power of Attorney

While a traditional will distributes a person's assets upon their death, a living will must be enforced while the person lives. It states under what circumstances you do not wish to be kept alive by extraordinary artificial life-support systems and authorizes doctors and named relatives to disconnect any equipment keeping you alive. A living will is activated when you become mentally or physically incapacitated and have no realistic hope of returning to your normal life.

Let's say mom, for example, becomes fatally ill or injured and can't make her own decisions or let her doctors know what kinds of life-prolonging medical care and treatment she does or doesn't want. Modern medicine and medical technology can keep her alive, sometimes indefinitely, whether the care and treatment she receives reflects her wishes or not. The cost of that care and treatment can deplete her estate and leave dad without resources. The emotional toll can be even more devastating. Planning for this possibility should be part of your parents' estate planning.

Anyone who has ever been in the hospital or had a relative or close friend hospitalized knows just how quickly the medical bills can add up. Even with good health insurance, a serious illness or accident can eat up a person's savings and maybe even force them to liquidate valuable assets, thus diminishing the size of their estate. This is especially true if a person is critically ill or injured and life-sustaining measures are used to keep you alive as long as possible.

An increasing number of people are dealing with this possibility by preparing health care directives, including a living will and a durable power of attorney for health care. Your parents can use these documents to control the kinds of health care and treatment they will receive if they are terminally ill or critically injured and can't speak for themselves. They may want to prepare health care directives for the following reasons:

1. They don't want to be kept alive at all costs, when there is no reasonable expectation of recovery.
2. They don't want their loved ones to go through the emotional pain of watching them die little by little.
3. They don't want to put their loved ones in the position of guessing about the kinds of health care and treatment they would or would not want

if they could speak for themselves. They especially don't want them to have to decide whether to end the care and treatment that is keeping them alive.

4. They want to spare their loved ones the time and expense involved in petitioning the court to have a conservator appointed to handle their affairs.

5. They don't want to see the assets in their estate depleted by costly medical care and treatment that they would not have selected were they able to make the decision themselves.

The federal government encourages the use of health care directives. For example, in 1990, Congress passed the Patient Self-Determination Act, which declares that any facility receiving Medicaid or Medicare monies must provide its patients with written information about health care directives at the time of their admission. It also says that if a person prepares a health care directive, the facility caring for that person must keep the document with the person's medical records. Many health care facilities provide their patients with standard forms for preparing their own living will and durable power of attorney for health care. This form must be updated regularly.

Most states now also recognize a person's right to die. Courts usually side with patients who have given explicit instructions in advance that they do not want their lives extended artificially. Valid living wills usually do not expire unless they are revoked. However, it's a good idea to review the document every five years or so. Initial and date it at each review to make sure readers know that it still reflects your wishes.

What Is a Living Will? A living will is a written document that speaks for a person if that person is too ill or too injured to speak for one's own self. It states the person's wishes regarding the use of various life-sustaining treatments and equipment, including respirators, breathing tubes, cardiac assist pumps, intravenous tubes, artificial nutrition tubes, artificial hydration, dialysis, cardiopulmonary resuscitation, and so on. Your parents' living wills can spell out what they do want as well as what they don't want. They can use it to provide their doctors with "do not resuscitate" instructions, "do all you can" instructions, or something in between. (The Web site http://www.agingwithdignity.org has a great form and booklet called "Five Wishes.")

Preparing a Living Will. Your parents can write their own living wills without the help of an attorney by using a living will fill-in-the-blanks form avail-

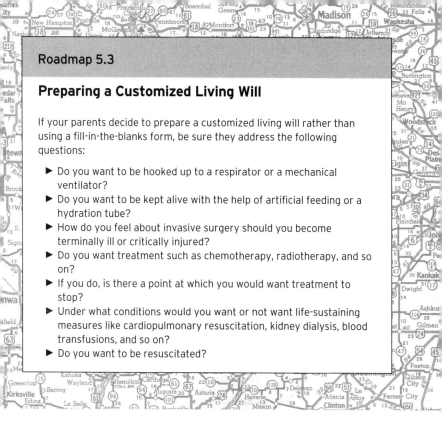

Roadmap 5.3

Preparing a Customized Living Will

If your parents decide to prepare a customized living will rather than using a fill-in-the-blanks form, be sure they address the following questions:

▶ Do you want to be hooked up to a respirator or a mechanical ventilator?

▶ Do you want to be kept alive with the help of artificial feeding or a hydration tube?

▶ How do you feel about invasive surgery should you become terminally ill or critically injured?

▶ Do you want treatment such as chemotherapy, radiotherapy, and so on?

▶ If you do, is there a point at which you would want treatment to stop?

▶ Under what conditions would you want or not want life-sustaining measures like cardiopulmonary resuscitation, kidney dialysis, blood transfusions, and so on?

▶ Do you want to be resuscitated?

able from a local hospital, bar association, or agency on aging. Also, several national nonprofit organizations offer living wills specific to each state.

Using a standard fill-in-the-blanks form is okay as long as it adheres to the laws of the state in which your parents live. If the form does not allow them to adequately address all of their concerns and preferences, they should have their living wills prepared by a qualified estate planning attorney. Roadmap 5.3 reviews the issues that should be addressed in that living will.

Sign your living will in front of two impartial adults who are not related to you, who stand to inherit nothing from you, and who are not doctors or hospital employees who might be in a position to disconnect your life-support equipment.

Once your parents have executed a living will, keep a copy of it with your medical records. It should be stored in a fireproof safe at home or in a safe-deposit box, and someone besides them should know the combination to the safe or have a key to the safe-deposit box. Also, each spouse should have a copy, as should a close family member, your primary physician, or a good friend. Also, they should give a copy of their living will to the executor of their estate. Your parents should review the document with these people so they can provide explanations of their wishes as necessary and so that person will feel comfortable if the living will has to be activated.

In most states, a person must let their doctor know that they have a living will. Even if that is not a requirement, reviewing their living wills with their doctor is an excellent idea. That way they can be sure that your doctor feels comfortable with the wishes stated in those wills. If their doctor does not feel comfortable, they can find a doctor who will enforce it. They should ask their doctor to keep a copy of their living wills with their medical records.

Legal Requirements for Living Wills. Living wills are recognized in all states. However, every state has its own criteria for what makes a living will legally valid and enforceable. The living will your parents prepare must also have certain characteristics to be legally valid.

1. You must be mentally competent at the time that you write your living will.
2. Your living will must be written; no state recognizes an oral living will.
3. Two adults must sign, date, and witness your living will. In most states, neither of the adults can be your legal heirs.
4. Your living will must be notarized.

Changing or Revoking a Living Will. Your parents can change or revoke their living wills whenever they wish. However, they must be sure you do it according to their state's rules for amendments and revocations.

In most states, all you need to do to revoke a living will is write on the document that it's no longer valid. If anyone has a copy of the living will you are invalidating, they should be sure to get those copies back. If the state in which they live requires registration of living wills, they should make sure they get that copy back as well.

When Will Your Parent's Living Will Be Activated? Generally, a living will cannot be activated until a person is near death and two doctors (sometimes one) have stated in writing that the person is unable to make their own decisions and is terminally ill or permanently unconscious. If a person is in a great deal of pain but death is not imminent, the living will won't go into effect.

Normally, if a person's doctor is aware that the person has a living will and if the document is legally valid, the doctor is expected to comply with it. However, it is always possible that your parent's doctor may ignore the directives or delay processing the paperwork required to activate it. Your doctor may do this for several reasons:

1. The doctor may be uncomfortable with the provisions in your living will.
2. The family does not want the living will to be activated and pressures the doctor not to follow the wishes expressed in it.
3. The two doctors who must state in writing that the person is terminally ill or permanently unconscious and near death disagree about the definition of those two terms, or they differ about your medical prognosis.
4. The provisions in your living will are too vague to be enforced.

To minimize the chance that the family will interfere with the activation of your parent's living will, it is important that family members read it after it's written, so that your parents can explain their requests, and answer any questions the family may have. If the family understands the thinking that went into their parents' living wills they are more apt to respect the wishes expressed in it.

If your parent is terminally ill or critically injured and the doctor will not comply with the directives in your parent's living will, you can ask that mom or dad be transferred to a more sympathetic physician. However, switching at this point can be difficult.

Durable Power of Attorney for Health Care. Giving someone a durable power of attorney for health care is one of the best things your parents can do to help ensure that their living wills are enforced when the time comes. The person who has the power of attorney can speak for your parent regarding their health care and treatment, and push to have your living will activated, if necessary. This person can also make medical and health decisions on your parent's behalf when they are dying. In some states, the person who holds durable power of attorney for health care can also make these same decisions when you are physically or mentally incapacitated but death is not an immediate threat. Therefore, a durable power of attorney for health care is a more comprehensive and powerful legal tool than a living will.

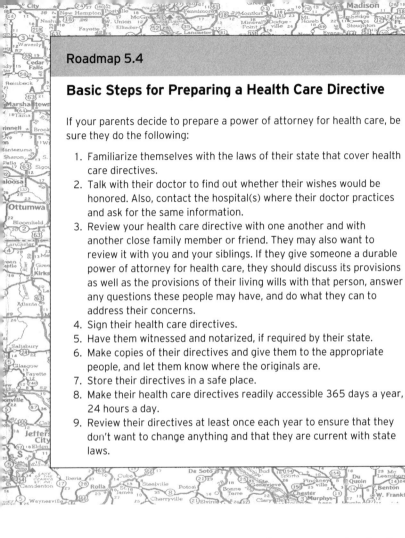

Roadmap 5.4

Basic Steps for Preparing a Health Care Directive

If your parents decide to prepare a power of attorney for health care, be sure they do the following:

1. Familiarize themselves with the laws of their state that cover health care directives.
2. Talk with their doctor to find out whether their wishes would be honored. Also, contact the hospital(s) where their doctor practices and ask for the same information.
3. Review your health care directive with one another and with another close family member or friend. They may also want to review it with you and your siblings. If they give someone a durable power of attorney for health care, they should discuss its provisions as well as the provisions of their living wills with that person, answer any questions these people may have, and do what they can to address their concerns.
4. Sign their health care directives.
5. Have them witnessed and notarized, if required by their state.
6. Make copies of their directives and give them to the appropriate people, and let them know where the originals are.
7. Store their directives in a safe place.
8. Make their health care directives readily accessible 365 days a year, 24 hours a day.
9. Review their directives at least once each year to ensure that they don't want to change anything and that they are current with state laws.

The person to whom your parents give this power must be a legal adult and, obviously, should be someone they trust implicitly and who they feel has the personal strength to make potentially difficult decisions on their behalf. Also, this person should be willing to accept the important responsibility your parents are entrusting.

Your parents should check with their state's attorney general's office or with the medical board in the state or county in which they live to find out whether there are any legal restrictions on the person to whom they grant a durable power of attorney for health care. For example, they may be prohibited from giving it to their doctor or their residential care provider.

The best kind of durable power of attorney for health care is one that not only specifies the kinds of medical care and treatment your parents do and don't want but also spells out their values and personal beliefs in regard to such things as life-sustaining measures, pain, the relative cost of various procedures and treatments, and other quality-of-life issues. They may also want to describe what they consider to be an acceptable quality of life. In their instructions to the person with the power of attorney, they should be as clear and specific as possible so that nothing is left to interpretation. Furthermore, they should talk about it with the individual to whom they give the power of attorney.

They can use a fill-in-the-blanks form as long as it meets your state's requirements. They can obtain it from the same organizations that provide a living will form. They can also hire an attorney to prepare a durable power of attorney for health care that reflects their particular needs and concerns.

Changing or Revoking a Durable Power of Attorney for Health Care. Your parents can change or revoke a durable power of attorney for health care whenever they wish, as long as they are mentally competent. If they change it, make sure they adhere to the laws of their state. If they revoke it, they should prepare a formal notice of revocation. Also, if they gave copies of your durable power of attorney for health care to other people, they should get them back and destroy them.

If You Don't Have a Living Will. If your parents become critically ill and they don't have a living will, the doctor in charge of their care will decide what treatment they will receive. Most likely, their doctor will do whatever is necessary to sustain their lives because that is the focus of your doctor's medical education and professional code of ethics. Furthermore, although their doctor may consult with your other parent and other close family members, the doctor is not obligated to comply with the family's wishes in the absence of a living will.

If your family wants to stop certain kinds of medical care and treatment because it believes that dad, for example, wouldn't want it but his doctor is not willing to comply, a court hearing may be held to resolve the stalemate. That hearing will involve legal costs and will no doubt be emotionally draining for them. Another option for the family is to find a new doctor more sympathetic to its wishes, which may again require involvement of the court. A third option is for the family to petition the court to have a conservator appointed who will make medical decisions for dad.

▶ Final Journey: Funeral Planning and Final Instructions

As distasteful as planning your parents' estate and executing their will may have been to them (and you), they probably dread even more the thought of making their funeral and burial arrangements. It is difficult enough to deal with the concept of your own demise when planning an estate, but it is often even harder to select burial plots, mausoleums, and caskets.

Yet someone must take care of these matters. Funerals and related items like burial plots can cost thousands of dollars, and the earlier they consider their options, the less money would be wasted. Strange as it may seem, they may also acquire peace of mind knowing what will happen when they die. It is a far better way to leave this earth than to have your family, already in deep emotional distress, trying to find a place to bury you and select a good funeral home.

The first decision your parents should make is what kind of final disposition they want for their remains. Knowing their wishes will give them and their survivors peace of mind. The funeral process is, after all, an emotional event that a person's spouse, children, relatives, and friends will remember long after the person has died.

Writing down their wishes regarding funeral arrangements or making their own arrangements can make things easier for the surviving spouse and family. In their written instructions, they should indicate whether they want to be buried or cremated and whether they want to donate their organs. They should also describe their funeral or memorial service—whom they want to speak, where it should be held, what music they want played, whom to invite, and so on. If they have purchased a burial plot and arranged for a casket, record that information too.

However your parents (or you and your family in the event your parents have not made the arrangements) choose to handle the funeral and burial, a good funeral director earns their fees by relieving the family of many details. The director transports the body to the funeral home, arranges for the wake (if appropriate), and gets information to the proper authorities for the death certificate. (The funeral director should obtain at least 10 certified copies of the death certificate; your survivors will need them for insurance companies, the probate court, Social Security offices, and other purposes.) The funeral director places obituary notices in newspapers and even helps fill out claim forms for Social Security survivors' benefits, veteran's benefits, and life insurance. The person also sets a time for the funeral and contacts clergy, if desired, to preside over the service. In addition, the funeral director explains options for various kinds of caskets and memorial tablets. On the day of the funeral, the director takes care of transportation and other logistics.

If your parents (or the family) are not careful, the cost of a funeral can add up quickly. For example, many funeral directors sell the entire funeral as a package, including items—such as pallbearers—that your parents and family may not want. They can obtain an itemized list of what the package includes and eliminate the expendables. Also, they should investigate the full range of alternatives, from the least expensive casket to the most elaborate. Funeral directors can also quote prices over the phone so your parents or family can comparison shop.

If your parents decide to prearrange their own funerals, your family will not have to raise the funds to cover burial and other expenses when they are least capable of doing so. This can be done with or without prepaying the expenses. Since funeral competition is heating up and prices in some areas going down, prepaying may not be the best plan. A Totten Trust—an individual savings plan earmarked for a person's funeral—can be established. While alive, the person controls the money, which is usually invested in a certificate of deposit or a money-market account. When your parent dies, the funds are available immediately to pay for the funeral.

Another such fund is a regulated trust, in which your parents' money is invested by the funeral home or cemetery to pay for their burials. They have no access to this money. This trust is enormously profitable for the funeral home or cemetery because it keeps the earnings that your parents' capital generates if the funeral costs less than the funds you deposited. The best prearranged packages will refund any unused money to your estate.

Before your parents sign up for a pre-funded funeral, find out whether they can get a total or partial refund if they change their minds about the package. For example, they might want to be buried in another state if they move from their current residence. Or they might not have the money to make the installment payments and want a refund of what they have already paid. They should also find out whether their current payment protects them against future price increases for funerals and related services. Most policies do, but they should make sure that theirs is one of them. In addition, they should find out what happens if the funeral home they are dealing with goes out of business. Normally, its contracts will be transferred to another home, but they should know which home that might be.

Funeral Consumer Alliance. One way to defray the high cost of funeral services is to join a local funeral consumer group once known as a memorial society. These organizations, which act as consumer advocates for funeral planning, are nonprofit, voluntary associations of people from all walks of life who support consumer choice for dignified, meaningful, affordable funerals.

Local societies can guide your parents to more affordable burial alternatives in their hometown. For example, it might not be necessary to use a funeral home to conduct a burial in their state. In other cases, memorial societies make arrangements with local undertakers to provide inexpensive funerals at a preset cost for members. When a person joins, they receive a prearrangement form allowing them to choose burial, cremation, or donation. If your parents choose this route, they can also describe the kind of service they want.

The Gift of Life: Organ Donation

The Uniform Anatomical Gift Act allows your parents to indicate whether they want their organs to be donated to others or to science after they die. Donating an organ so that someone else may live is perhaps the greatest gift one person can give to another.

If organ donation is your parents' desire, it is a good idea to obtain an organ donor card from your state's department of motor vehicles. They should complete the card, have it witnessed, and keep it with them at all times. Their donation wishes are printed on the back of their driver's license or other ID obtained from state motor vehicles departments. They should also make sure that their doctor, close family members, and the person with the durable power of attorney for their health care are aware of their organ donation plans. The surviving spouse or another close family member must sign a form consenting to the donation. If that family member is unaware of your wishes or disagrees with them, the person might refuse to sign the form.

Travelogue: Where to Find Important Documents

Many wills simply divide estates into bulk portions, mentioning major assets but leaving heirs, executors, and the courts to determine the remaining contents of the deceased's estate. Without clear records, the family is faced with the burdensome and often costly task of locating records, papers, and documents to establish the content and value of the estate. Furthermore, certain major assets are not even typically included in wills. Life insurance proceeds, pensions, Social Security, and veteran's benefits, for example, all have fixed plans of distribution unaffected by wills, and so they are not commonly mentioned in them. Therefore, a clear, up-to-date, comprehensive listing of all of your parents' available assets and their benefits can be invaluable to you and your family and other heirs. What to Pack on pages 133–135 offers an easy-to-prepare form that your parents can complete and update as circumstances change. They should keep copies of originals in your home filing system.

Souvenirs: Personal History

Perhaps the most cherished legacy your parents can provide you and your family is their unique knowledge of your family's history; in other words their recollections about their own lives, interests, accomplishments, and other special remembrances. Encourage both parents to write it down or make a cassette or CD; you might even decide to make a video of them. Other family members might want to participate by asking questions about various aspects of your past. Whichever way you and your parents do it, we strongly suggest you do it.

After all, no one knows the family's history as well as they do. If they don't know where to begin, you might start them off with questions like these:

▶ Where were you born?
▶ Where did you go to school?
▶ In what cities you have lived?
▶ What is your mother's family name?
▶ Where did your parents live or where are they buried?
▶ What kinds of work experiences have you had?
▶ Tell us about the hobbies and clubs you have enjoyed through the years.

What to Pack

Where to Find Records and Keys

Personal History	Other Locations

Safe-Deposit Box

- ▶ Adoption papers
- ▶ Annulment decrees or judgments
- ▶ Athletic awards
- ▶ Birth certificates
- ▶ Change of name certificates
- ▶ Civic awards
- ▶ Death certificates
- ▶ Divorce decrees or judgments
- ▶ Dramatic awards
- ▶ Educational certificates
- ▶ Educational transcripts
- ▶ Marriage certificates
- ▶ Military awards
- ▶ Military separation papers
- ▶ Naturalization papers
- ▶ Newspaper articles
- ▶ Organization awards
- ▶ Organization membership certificates
- ▶ Other _____

    _____

    _____

Insurance

- ▶ Life insurance policies
- ▶ Medical and health insurance policies
- ▶ Residence insurance policies
- ▶ Vehicle insurance policies
- ▶ Other _____

    _____

    _____

Other Benefits

- ▶ 401(k) agreements
- ▶ IRA agreements
- ▶ Keogh plan agreements
- ▶ Medicare card

Other Benefits (*continued*)

▶ Military separation papers _____

▶ Pension agreements _____

▶ Railroad retirement documents _____

▶ Social Security card _____

▶ Workers' compensation award _____

▶ Copies of beneficiary designations _____

▶ Other _____ _____

_____

_____

Banking and Savings

▶ Cash _____

▶ Checking account statements _____

▶ Credit union account statements _____

▶ Savings account books or statements _____

▶ Copies of beneficiary designations _____

▶ Other _____ _____

_____

_____

**Securities, Real Estate, and
Miscellaneous Assets**

▶ Business records _____

▶ Decrees _____

▶ Deeds _____

▶ Home improvement records _____

▶ Judgments _____

▶ Leases _____

▶ Mortgages _____

▶ Patents or copyrights _____

▶ Rental property records _____

▶ Stock brokerage statements _____

▶ Vehicle certificates of title _____

▶ Copies of beneficiary designations _____

▶ Other _____ _____

_____

_____

Will, Trust Agreements, etc. (Originals)

▶ Living will _____

▶ Powers of attorney _____

▶ Durable power of attorney for financial
management _____

▶ Durable power of attorney for health care _____

	Locations

Will, Trust Agreements, etc. (Originals)
(*continued*)
▶ Other powers of attorney _____
▶ Trust agreement _____
▶ Will and codicils _____
▶ Other _____ _____
_____
_____

Final Wishes (Originals)
▶ Body bequeathal papers _____
▶ Cemetery deed _____
▶ Funeral prearrangement agreement _____
▶ Funeral prepayment agreement _____
▶ Mausoleum deed _____
▶ Uniform donor card _____
▶ Other _____ _____
_____
_____

Miscellaneous Information
▶ Animal care information _____
▶ Burglar alarm information _____
▶ Child care information _____
▶ Letters to be sent upon my death _____
▶ List of hiding places for valuables _____
▶ Property care information _____
▶ Tax records _____
▶ Other _____ _____
_____
_____

Keys and Combinations
▶ Keys to homes _____
▶ Keys to other real estate _____
▶ Keys to post office boxes _____
▶ Keys to safe-deposit box(es) _____
▶ Keys to vehicles _____
▶ Other keys _____
▶ List of combinations to locks _____
▶ Other _____
▶ Passcode to online service(s) _____
▶ Cassettes _____
▶ Computer and other electronic media _____

▶ Photos _____

▶ Videos/movies _____

▶ Other _____ _____

_____ _____

_____ _____

Most of us become more interested in family history as we age, but if someone does not record the facts of that history for us, they will be lost. To fill in gaps in their own knowledge, suggest they telephone, drop a note, or e-mail a brother, sister, aunt, uncle, son, or daughter and gradually fill in the blanks in their family's history. As a bonus, they might even rekindle family ties!

Appendix A

An Itinerary

Here's a quick review of what to do, as you set out on the road to caring for an aging parent:

Stop #1. If possible, the best way to approach caring for a parent (and to relieve some of the anxiety you, your parent, and other family members may have) is to discuss the situation openly. In that way your parent or parents can help plan for their needs well before they ever arise. Discuss finances, living arrangements, and healthcare, as well as estate planning, legal, and other related issues.

▶ Note (Roadmap 1.2) where all the important documents of your parent's are located and other details such as account numbers and the names of brokers, insurance agents, and other people who know about their accounts.
▶ Evaluate each aspect of your parent(s)' personal finances so you can understand where mom or dad stand and what help they might need going forward.

   1. How much income do they receive from pensions, IRAs, Keoghs, salary reduction plans, annuities, Social Security, and investment portfolio?
   2. Estimate their living expenses in retirement, or, if already retired, how much are they spending?
   3. Draw up a realistic budget based on the assets they have, the income those assets can generate, and their expenses.

▶ Begin a discussion of your parent's current and present housing needs.
▶ Use Roadmap 1.2 to create a family medical history; this will be important for both your parent and other members of their family in assessing medical needs and risks.

▶ Begin a discussion of estate planning. Note that estate planning includes plans for health care issues as well as the management and disposition of your parent's money and personal property.

▶ Every parent's and family's needs are different; initiate regular family meetings to discuss present and future needs.

Stop #2. Achieving financial security in one's retirement years has never been more important. Advances in modern medicine commonly extends lives into the 80s, 90s, and even 100s. Is your parent financially prepared?

▶ Use Roadmaps 2.1 and 2.2 to analyze your parent's assets and liabilities. By doing this exercise, you will be able to determine how well prepared or unprepared they are.

▶ Then use Roadmap 2.3 to analyze your parent's current cash flow, meaning where is the money coming from and where is it going.

▶ With this information in hand, you can begin assembling a realistic long-term plan and to calculate how much money your parent will need in retirement and to pinpoint their potential sources of income. Roadmap 2.4 will guide you through these calculations.

1. Does your parent have enough in savings and investments and other sources of income to last?
2. How should your parent safely draw down their portfolio to ensure that the nest egg lasts as long as they are alive?
3. Which types of accounts should the money be taken from first?
4. If your parent's money is insufficient, it's time to analyze the options.

▶ Analyze your parent's assets to make certain that they are providing an appropriate income stream to meet their needs and to determine whether or not they are properly invested and allocated.

▶ Assess whether funds are being withdrawn to minimize tax impact and maximize growth. Plan a withdrawal plan from tax-deferred accounts such as IRAs and 401(k)s to minimize tax bite. Make certain your parent is taking full advantage of the many provisions in the tax code aimed at senior citizens.

▶ Social Security Planning:

  1. If you are doing advance planning, and your parent is not yet receiving Social Security, analyze the pros and cons of taking early retirement.

  2. Is your parent eligible for Supplemental Security Income?

▶ Has your parent applied for all company pension benefits to which they are entitled? If your parent is unsure, it's wise to check with all former employers to make certain no money is being held in your parent's retirement account. What about veteran's benefits?

▶ Take a look at life insurance policies and annuities. Would it make sense to convert a life insurance policy into an annuity or perhaps convert it to cash? Or would it be best to leave it as is and let it accumulate cash value?

▶ It's now time to create a written budget (Roadmaps 2.5 and 2.6), which will help you and your parent understand priorities, may motivate your parent to take charge of their financial life, and provide the comfort that comes from knowing they are in control.

▶ It is very possible that your parent has equity built up in their home. If after all the calculations are done, it is decided that your parent can no longer afford to live in the home, the time may have come to sell it or, perhaps, to withdraw equity from it either by refinancing or through a reverse mortgage.

  1. If your parent decides to sell use Roadmap 2.7 to determine how much mom or dad will net from the sale.

  2. Before refinancing or taking out a reverse mortgage, examine all of your parent's options; Roadmap 2.7 will help you determine if refinancing makes sense.

▶ Viatical settlements are an option of last resort if your parent is terminally ill and in need of cash and has life insurance coverage.

Stop #3. As part of your parents' retirement plans, they might consider moving to a new area or to a smaller, less demanding home or renovating their current home. They should consider their housing alternatives now and for the longer term. In addition to finances, among the factors they must consider are the following:

1. What if one or both of them become ill; what if one dies? Do they want to plan for those eventualities or are they willing and able to make another move?
2. What sort of lifestyle do they want?
3. Where do they want to live?

▶ Assuming your parents have decided to make the family home their retirement home, some other things that should be considered include:

1. How to make their home safer and more comfortable for them as they age.
2. Do they now need or will they need people to cut the grass, wash the windows, cook meals, do the shopping, provide personal care and/or skilled nursing care?
3. If your parent is alone, would they take in a boarder, who would share the home much as youngsters do when they find a roommate to share an apartment? Or should a family member move in or should your parent move in with a family member? What about adding an "in-law" apartment? (Note: Some of these arrangements might also provide extra income along with a sense of well-being.)

▶ Assuming your parents have decided to move, there are many issues to consider. Roadmap 3.2 provides an extensive list of questions to ask about the community and area as well as about the type of home they are considering. They should also consider whether to buy or rent their new home.
▶ What kind of housing will best serve their needs, both today and in the future? Options include:

1. single family home, co-op, condominium, or town home
2. retirement community
3. manufactured home park
4. assisted living or continuing care retirement community
5. nursing facility

Each must be carefully evaluated based on your parent's needs.

Stop #4. It is crucial that you and your parent(s) understand their health insurance options and maximize their benefits at the least possible cost.

Adequate health insurance is critical because your parent(s) can easily be devastated financially if they need major surgery or long-term medical care.

▶ For those age 65 or older, Medicare provides substantial health insurance benefits—whether your parent is retired or still working.

▶ Medicare Part A covers hospital expenses. Coverage is automatic. Part B coverage is elective and requires that the recipient pay a monthly premium as well as deductibles, and coinsurance. It covers hospitalization, surgery, doctor bills, home health care, and skilled nursing care considered to be medically necessary and *within reasonable cost limits.*

▶ Your parent should also explore participating in the Medicare Advantage Plan or a Medigap Plan, which cover medical services not covered by Medicare. To participate, your parents must also be covered by Medicare Parts A and B. What plan your parent should choose depends on lifestyle and personal economics. Does your parent plan to travel? Some plans will cover him or her outside the United States. Other plans may limit prescription benefits. Cost—now and in the future—is the primary consideration.

▶ Medicare does not cover prescription drugs. If your parent has no other insurance, and depending on your parent's drug costs, even if the other plan does cover prescription drugs, investigate Medicare's prescription drug plan.

▶ Your parent and you should carefully consider whether or not a long-term care policy makes sense. Understanding long-term care insurance can be a challenge because each company and policy has its own features and benefits. The policies are expensive, but so is the cost of care. Get the *Understanding Long Term Care Insurance* brochure from the National Association of Insurance Commissioners (http://www.naic. org). Your parent should probably buy long-term care insurance if they can afford it and want to maintain their independence, retain more control over (and your) care choices and the quality of care, or preserve as much as possible of the income and assets. Your parent should not buy it if they cannot afford the premium now or in the future; has limited assets, has only Social Security or Supplemental Security Income as an income source, has trouble paying for utilities, rent, food, medicine, or other important needs, or can afford and prefers to pay care costs out of pocket, if needed.

▶ Decisions associated with buying long-term care insurance include:

1. Where does your parent want their care to take place?
2. For how long do they want to receive benefits?
3. How much money do they want as a daily benefit?
4. How long does dad want to wait after he starts receiving care for the insurance benefits to begin?
5. What, if any, protection from inflation does he want?

▶ Medicaid provides medical care to the elderly, blind, and disabled poor; unlike Medicare, eligibility for Medicaid is based on financial need. Medicaid provides a safety net for long-term nursing care for those who cannot afford it. Applications for Medicaid coverage are made with the appropriate state agency. Substantial documentation and paperwork are required. To qualify for Medicaid, your parent must exhaust all other assets except in some cases the house, car, and household belongings.

Stop #5. Hard as it is to think and talk about, estate planning and related subjects, like living wills and healthcare directives, are issues you and your parents must confront. Estate planning is an ongoing process; something both parents should plan for before either becomes ill and which should continue for the remainder of each of their lives. How they plan will affect the lives of the widow(er) and may, if you become responsible for the care of one or both parents, affect your life as well.

▶ Whether they do it themselves or with the help of legal advisors, executing a will is key to estate planning. Other rights and benefits, like pension rights and life insurance proceeds, are normally handled by beneficiary designation, which takes precedence over a will.
▶ A document that functions much like a will is a Revocable Living Trust (Inter Vivos Trust). The primary benefits of living trusts are ease of asset/property transfer and probate avoidance. This saves time, money, and hassles.
▶ They should also execute a financial power of attorney, or durable power of attorney for finance, which provides for the appointment of a person(s) to make financial decisions for each of your parents. This power may go into effect immediately on signing the document, or it may be delayed until an event occurs that triggers the power or until your parent is unable to manage their own financial affairs. As with all financial and legal decisions, it is important that your parents carefully consider to whom they give this power.

▶ For most people, the odds of becoming medically or mentally incapacitated at any given moment are actually higher than the odds of dying. It is also possible that a person may become physically or mentally incapacitated for a limited period and unable to manage their own affairs. For this reason, your parents should also execute the appropriate medical documents, which generally include the following:

1. A directive to physicians, telling medical personnel what, if any, means of artificial life support you would want and under what circumstances, in the event of your medical incapacity. Roadmap 5.3 will guide your parents through the questions your parents may wish to address. The living will your parents prepare must also have certain characteristics to be legally valid.

   ▶ They must be mentally competent at the time that you write your living will.
   ▶ Their living will must be written; no state recognizes an oral living will.
   ▶ Two adults must sign, date, and witness your living will. In most states, neither of the adults can be your legal heirs.
   ▶ Your living will must be notarized.

2. A Durable Power of Attorney for Healthcare, which names someone to make medical decisions if your parents can't, and who will help ensure that their living wills are enforced if necessary. The person who has the power of attorney can speak for your parents regarding their health care and treatment.

▶ Your parents should also write down their wishes regarding funeral arrangements and/or make their own arrangements. This can make things easier for the surviving spouse and family.

▶ They should consider establishing a Totten Trust, which is an individual savings plan earmarked for a person's funeral. While the person lives, they control the money, which is usually invested in a certificate of deposit or a money-market account. When your parent dies, the funds are available immediately to pay for the funeral.

▶ Another such fund is a regulated trust, in which your parents' money is invested by the funeral home or cemetery to pay for their burials. You have no access to this money. The best prearranged packages will refund any unused money to your estate. Before your parents sign up for a pre-funded funeral, find out whether they can get a total or partial refund if they change their minds about the package. They should also find out whether their current payment protects them against future price increases for funerals and related services.

▶ The Uniform Anatomical Gift Act allows your parents to indicate whether they want their organs to be donated to others or to science after they die. Donating an organ so that someone else may live is perhaps the greatest gift one person can give to another. If organ donation is your parents' desire, it is a good idea to obtain an organ donor card from your state's department of motor vehicles. They should complete the card, have it witnessed, and keep it with them at all times.

▶ A clear, up-to-date, comprehensive listing of all of your parents' available assets and their benefits can be invaluable to you and your family and other heirs. What to Pack on pages 132–135 offers an easy-to-prepare form that your parents can complete and update as circumstances change.

▶ Perhaps the most cherished legacy your parents can provide you and your family is their unique knowledge of your family's history: their recollections about their own lives, interests, accomplishments, and other special remembrances. Encourage both parents to write it down or make a cassette or CD; you might even decide to make a video of them.

Appendix B
The Best of *Caring for an Aging Parent*: A Resource Guide

▶ Bibliography

The following books were used as resources for this book. In addition, we have provided lists of other books and Web sites that offer more detailed information on some of the topics covered in this book. We hope you find all these resources useful.

Garrett, Sheryl. *Just Give Me the Answers: Expert Advisors Address Your Most Pressing Financial Questions.* Chicago: Dearborn Trade Publishing, 2004.

Goodman, Jordan E. *Everyone's Money Book,* 3rd ed. Chicago: Dearborn Trade Publishing, 2001.

Lawrence, Judy. *The Budget Kit,* 4th ed. Chicago: Dearborn Trade Publishing, 2004.

Lewis, Allyson, CFP. *The Million Dollar Car and $250,000 Pizza.* Chicago: Dearborn Trade Publishing, 2000.

Magee, David S. and John Ventura. *Everything Your Heirs Need to Know.* Chicago: Dearborn Trade Publishing, 1999.

Ventura, John. *The Will Kit,* 2nd ed. Chicago: Dearborn Trade Publishing, 2002.

▶ Recommended Books and Web Sites
For Chapter 1, Facing the Future Together
Books

▶ *Bankroll Your Future: How to Get the Most from Uncle Sam for Your Retirement Years—Social Security, Medicare, and Much More* by Ellen Hoffman (Newmarket Press, 18 East 48th Street, New York, NY 10017;

Telephone: 212-832-3575; http://www.newmarketpress.com). For each of the following topics covers what you need to know; the decisions you need to make; the tax factor; and where to find more information: Social Security, medicare, long-term care, pensions, nursing home care, job security/age discrimination laws, retirement home, consumer protection, and tax laws.

▶ *You've Earned It, Don't Lose It: Mistakes You Can't Afford to Make When You Retire* by Suze Orman (Newmarket Press, 18 East 48th Street, New York, NY 10017; Telephone: 212-832-3575; http://www.newmarketpress. com). Overview of investment advice and what to look for in an investment counselor, includes focused discussions of trusts vs. wills, long-term care insurance, early retirement, durable power of attorney, estate taxes and probate costs, minimizing your expenses/maximizing your income, joint and survivor benefits, and a successful retirement.

▶ *How to Care For Your Parents' Money While Caring for Your Parents* by Sharon Burns, Raymond Forgue (The McGraw-Hill Companies, P.O. Box 182604, Columbus, OH 43272; Telephone: 877-833-5524; http://www. mcgraw-hill.com). In this guide, two family finance experts who are caring for their own parents' finances provide a basic primer in personal finance for those who are involved in their parents' financial lives.

▶ *Suddenly Single: Money Skills for Divorcees and Widows,* by Kerry Hannon (John Wiley & Sons, 10475 Crosspoint Blvd., Indianapolis, IN 46256; Telephone: 877-762-2974; 800-225-5945; http://www.wiley.com). Resource for handling investments, taxes and legal impediments; investing, estate planning, saving for retirement.

Associations

▶ American Association of Retired Persons (AARP, 601 E St., N.W., Washington, DC 20049; Telephone: 202-434-2277; 800-424-3410; http://www. aarp.org). Represents people nearing retirement and those who have retired. Offers to its members credit cards, discount drug purchase programs, educational seminars, insurance, mutual funds, travel opportunities, and many other services as well as free publications on a wide variety of subjects.

▶ National Council on the Aging (300 D Street, SW, Suite 801, Washington, D.C. 20024; Telephone: 202-479-1200, http://www.ncoa.org). A nonprofit group specializing in setting standards for operating senior centers and adult day centers; also lobbies on various issues and offers programs in a variety of areas.

▶ Children of Aging Parents (1609 Woodbourne Rd., Suite 302A, Levittown, PA 19057; Telephone: 215-945-6900; http://www.experts.com). A national clearinghouse for information resources and support for caregivers of the elderly and allied health professionals. Sponsors a helpline and support groups and publishes a newsletter helpful to those having problems with an elderly relative.

▶ Older Women's League (1750 New York Ave. NW, Suite 350, Washington, DC 20006; Telephone: 202-783-6686, 800-825-3695 http://www.owl-national.org/index.htm). A group dedicated to the interests of midlife and older women. Publishes the *Owl Observer,* which tracks issues such as health insurance and pension rights; also offers several pamphlets and books of interest to older women.

Web sites

▶ Administration on Aging (including the National Aging Information Center). Provides links to government agencies, professional associations, and many other information sources covering health care, financial benefit programs, elder law, and advocacy groups who work on behalf of seniors. Web site: http://www.aoa.dhhs.gov/default.htm

▶ Careguide.com. Contains articles and directories for senior services, such as financial planning, legal planning, senior care facility location and evaluation services, options for paying for care, and links to financial and legal advisors; also has online support groups. http://www.eldercare.com

For Chapter 2: Budgeting for Now and the Future
Books

▶ *Retirement Bible* by Lynn O'Shaughnessy (John Wiley and Sons, 10475 Crosspoint Blvd., Indianapolis, IN 46256; Telephone: 877-762-2974; 800-225-5945; http://www.wiley.com). A guide to the personal finance issues surrounding retirement, from 401(k)s to estate planning and trusts.

▶ *Retire on Less Than You Think: The New York Times Guide to Planning Your Financial Future* by Fred Brock (Times Books, Henry Holt and Company, Inc., 115 West 18th Street, New York, NY 10011; Telephone:

212-886-9200, http://www.henryholt.com/timesbooks.htm) Based on current and projected savings, it may be just as easy to cut back and simplify lifestyles, whether that means moving to a less expensive area or streamlining postretirement activities or both.

► *Set for Life: Financial Peace for People over 50* by Bambi Holzer (John Wiley & Sons, 10475 Crosspoint Blvd., Indianapolis, IN 46256; Telephone: 877-762-2974; 800-225-5945; http://www.wiley.com). Provides straightforward, practical advice; shows how to manage money, cope with taxes and insurance, stay on top of inflation, and plan for the ultimate disposition of their estates.

Associations

► Legal Counsel for the Elderly (Building A, 601 E St., N.W., 4th Floor, Washington, DC 20049; Telephone: 202-434-2120; http://www.aarp.org/lce). A nonprofit legal support center, sponsored by AARP, dealing with issues of concern to the elderly. Offers legal services by referring the consumer to a local "Legal Counsel for the Elderly" attorney, whose services for the first 30 minutes of consultation are free.

► National Academy of Elder Law Attorneys, Inc. (1604 N. Country Club Rd., Tucson, AZ 85716; Telephone: 520-881-4005; http://www.naela.org). Offers a directory of lawyers specializing in problems faced by retirees. Will send the free booklet *Questions and Answers When Looking for an Elder Law Attorney.*

► National Organization of Social Security Claimants' Representatives (560 Sylvan Ave, Englewood Cliffs, NJ 07632; Telephone: 800-431-2804; http://www.nosscr.org). A group of lawyers who specialize in resolving disability and SSI benefits claims problems with the Social Security Administration. Call the toll-free telephone number for a referral to a specialized lawyer near your home.

► National Pension Lawyers Network (Gerontology Institute, University of Massachusetts Boston, 100 Morrissey St., Boston, MA 02125-3393; Telephone: 617-287-7332; http://www.pensionaction.org/npln.htm). A national lawyer referral service for workers, retirees, widows, and people going through divorce who need legal representation in cases involving pension issues. Also provides technical assistance on pension issues to other attorneys. To receive a listing of lawyers in a particular state, check the Web site or contact the institute.

▶ National Senior Citizens Law Center (1101 14th St., N.W., Suite 400, Washington, DC 20005; Telephone: 202-289-6976; http://www.nsclc. org). Lawyers' group that lobbies for legal services programs on behalf of the elderly; specializes in litigation, research, lobbying, and training lawyers on issues of concern to retired people. Subjects covered include age discrimination, guardianship, home care, mandatory retirement, Medicaid, Medicare, nursing homes, pensions, Social Security, and SSI. Offers publications and newsletters on all these topics.

▶ Pension Rights Center (1350 Connecticut Ave. NW, Suite 206, Washington, DC 20036; Telephone: 202-296-3778; http://www.pensionrights.org). A nonprofit organization that helps educate the public about pension issues. Offers a lawyer referral service for pension-related problems.

▶ *Annuity Shopper* (United States Annuities, 8 Talmadge Dr., Monroe Twp., NJ 08831; Telephone: 908-521-5110; 800-872-6684; http://www. annuityshopper.com). The newsletter compares the current rates paid by most immediate annuities, as well as the returns on fixed and variable annuities.

Web sites

▶ Morningstar.com. Good site to research mutual funds and stocks. Lots of mutual fund information available on this site. http://www.morningstar. com

▶ National Center for Home Equity Conversion Mortgage (NCHEC) http:// www.reverse.org

For Chapter 3, Choosing the Right Place to Live
Books

▶ *Retire in Style: 60 Outstanding Places Across the USA and Canada* by Warren R. Bland (Next Decade, Inc, 39 Old Farmstead Road, Chester, NJ 07930; Telephone: 800-595-5440, http://www.nextdecade.com). Guides retirees toward outstanding places to spend their golden years; based on 12 criteria—landscape, climate, quality of life, cost of living, transportation, retail services, health care, community services, cultural activities, recreational activities, work/volunteer activities, and crime; also includes a city map and climatic table.

Associations

▶ National Center for Home Equity Conversion (360 N. Robert, #403, St. Paul, MN 55101; Telephone: 651-222-6775; http://www.reverse.org). This is a nonprofit organization established to educate consumers about reverse mortgages.

Federal Regulators

▶ Pension Benefit Guaranty Corporation (1200 K St., N.W., Washington, DC 20005; Telephone: 202-326-4000; 800-400-7242; http://www.pbgc. gov). Protects the retirement incomes of about 43 million American workers—in nearly 40,000 defined benefit pension plans. A defined benefit plan provides a specified monthly benefit at retirement, often based on a combination of salary and years of service.

▶ Social Security Administration (6401 Security Blvd., Baltimore, MD 21235; Telephone: 410-965-7700; 800-772-1213; http://www.ssa.gov). Regulates distribution of Social Security benefits to eligible, retired, or disabled Americans; also administers programs for the aged, the blind, and dependents. Call for a free copy of the *Social Security Handbook* and any one of over 100 free booklets and pamphlets on a variety of Social Security, disability, Medicare, SSI, retirement, and other related subjects. You can also download them from the Web site or write to Public Information Distribution Center (Social Security Administration, P.O. Box 17743, Baltimore, MD 21235; Telephone: 410-965-0945).

For Chapter 4, Healthcare

Books

▶ *The New Nursing Homes: A 20-Minute Way to Find Great Long-Term Care* by Marylin Rantz, Lori Popejoy, and Mary Zwygart-Stauffacher (Fairview Press, 2450 Riverside Ave., Minneapolis, MN 55454; Telephone: 800-544-8207; http://www.fairviewpress.org/). Focuses on new nursing homes that emphasize quality of life, and offer many more amenities, such as pets, plants, consistent staff assignments, and teamwork. Also, rehabilitation that helps older people regain strength and skills so they can go back to live in their house or apartment.

Associations

▶ Aging Network Services (4400 East West Hwy., Suite 907, Bethesda, MD 20814; Telephone: 301-657-4329; http://www.agingnets.com). Provides referrals to social workers specializing in caring for the aged.

▶ American Association of Homes and Services for the Aging (American Association of Homes and Services for the Aging, 2519 Connecticut Ave., NW, Washington, DC 20008; Telephone: 202-783-2242; http://www.aahsa.org). Helps the elderly find appropriate housing, tracks the accreditation for health facilities, and can recommend well-run communities.

▶ American Health Care Association (1201 L St., N.W., Washington, DC 20005; Telephone: 202-842-4444; http://www.ahca.org). The AHCA is a federation of 50 state health organizations, representing nearly 12,000 nonprofit and for-profit assisted living, nursing facility, long-term-care, and sub-acute-care providers that care for more than one million elderly and disabled individuals nationally.

▶ Eldercare Locator (1112 16th St., N.W., Suite 100, Washington, DC 20036; Telephone: 1-800-677-1116, http://www.eldercare.gov/Eldercare/Public/Home.asp). Referral service for adult day care, home-delivered meals, transportation, home health care, and local centers for seniors.

▶ Medicare Rights Center (1460 Broadway, 11th Floor, New York, NY 10036; Telephone: 212-869-3850; http://www.medicarerights.org). Established to provide free counseling services to people with Medicare questions or problems. Conducts training programs and presentations for other senior and Medicare-related organizations.

▶ National Alliance for Caregiving (4720 Montgomery Ln., Suite 642, Bethesda, MD 20814; http://www.caregiving.org). This is a nonprofit joint venture that supports family caregivers of the elderly and the professionals who serve them. There are three NAC partners: The American Society on Aging, the Department of Veterans Affairs, and the National Association of Area Agencies on Aging, and founding sponsor Glaxo Wellcome. The Alliance was created to conduct research, develop national projects, and increase public awareness of the issues of family caregiving.

▶ National Association of Professional Geriatric Care Managers (1604 N. Country Club Rd., Tucson, AZ 85716; Telephone: 520-881-8008; http://www.caremanager.org). Locates certified professionals who assess and coordinate financial, legal, and medical care needs of elderly clients and their families.

▶ National Family Caregivers Association (10400 Connecticut Ave., Suite 500, Kensington, MD 20895; Telephone: 301-942-6430; 800-896-3650; http://www.nfcacares.org). A membership aimed at improving the overall quality of life of America's caregivers and educating the public about the difficulties caregivers face. Offers a newsletter and national speakers' bureau.

Federal Regulator

▶ The Health Care Financing Administration (7500 Security Blvd., Baltimore, MD 21244; Telephone: 410-786-3000; http://www.cms.hhs.gov). This federal agency oversees Medicare and Medicaid funding. The agency offers extensive information about nursing homes.

▶ AAHSA, 2519 Connecticut Ave., NW, Washington, DC 20008; Telephone: 202-783-2242; fax 202.783.2255 http://www.aahsa.org

Web sites

▶ Medicare benefits, rules, and limitations constantly change. To get the most current information, visit the Medicare Web site (http://www.medicare.gov) or call 800-633-4227.

▶ Caregiving Online. Site is associated with the newsletter *Caregiving*; offers online discussions for home caregivers and makes available an online journal of personal stories. http://www.caregiving.com

▶ Centerwatch. Lists clinical trials by condition and geographic location, and invites patients to participate; in some cases, there are cash awards available to participants. http://www.centerwatch.com

▶ Coalition for Medicare Choices. Organization of seniors advocating quality health care and expanded health plan choices for Medicare beneficiaries. Provides links to Congress to make your concerns known. http://www.medicarechoices.org

▶ ElderCare Online. Offers information on how to care for the elderly, medical issues, home care and independent living, insurance, legal and financial matters, longevity and wellness, and transitions. http://www.ec-online.net

▶ Extendedcare.com. This site provides links for consumers, hospitals, and extended care providers. For consumers, whether seniors or those taking

care of seniors, the site has links to some 75,000 providers. http://www.
extendedcare.com

▶ HealthGrades.com. This site rates and grades hospitals, physicians, health
plans, nursing homes, home health agencies, hospice programs, chiro-
practors, dentists, acupuncturists, assisted living programs, and birth
centers. http://www.healthgrades.com

▶ Intelihealth. Johns Hopkins University and Aetna U.S. Healthcare's site
with questions on common ailments answered by the center's world-class
doctors. http://www.intelihealth.com

▶ Medlineplus. Comprehensive medical and drug information site. http://
www.medlineplus.gov

▶ National Institutes of Health. Gateway to the resources of federal agencies, including a list of diseases being studied by various institutions;
offers medical publications and fact sheets online. http://www.nih.gov/
health

▶ United Seniors Health Cooperative. A nonprofit organization compris-
ing consumers, advocates, and elder care professionals with a mission to
provide up-to-date, unbiased, and accurate information and community
services and resources to consumers. http://www.ushc-online.org.

For Chapter 5: Estate Planning, and Other Hard-to-Discuss Topics

Books

▶ *AARP Crash Course in Estate Planning: The Essential Guide to Wills,
Trusts, and Your Personal Legacy* Michael T. Palermo (Sterling Publishing
Co., Inc., 387 Park Avenue South, New York, New York 10016; Telephone:
212-532-7160, http://www.sterlingpub.com). Walks readers through the
entire process, from understanding the distinction between probate and
non-probate property to delegating a durable power of attorney, and from
resolving possible tax issues ahead of time to safeguarding your assets.

▶ *The American Bar Association Guide to Wills and Estates, 2nd ed.: Everything You Need to Know About Wills, Estates, Trusts, and Taxes* by
American Bar Association (Random House Reference, 1745 Broadway,
New York, NY 10019; Telephone: 212-782-9000; http://www.randomhouse.
com) An overview of the law of estate planning; provides explanations
of wills, trusts, and living trusts and covers essential information like
choosing an executor, dealing with taxes, and planning for disability;

estate-planning checklist allows readers to evaluate their own situations to create or update their estate plan.

▶ *Beyond the Grave: The Right Way and the Wrong Way of Leaving Money to Your Children (And Others)* by Gerald M. Condon and Jeffrey L. Condon (HarperBusiness, P.O. Box 588, Dunmore, PA 18512; Telephone: 212-207-7000; 800-331-3761; http://www.harpercollins.com). Guide to estate planning, written by lawyers, explains how to provide fairly and equitably for family members, facilitate charitable bequests, and avoid probate.

▶ *Caring for the Dead: Your Final Act of Love* by Lisa Carlson (Upper Access Press, P.O. Box 457, Hinesburg, VT 05461; Telephone: 800-356-9315). A comprehensive guide to arranging a low-cost but dignified funeral, written by the executive director of the Funeral and Memorial Societies of America. Also lists all the laws pertaining to the funeral industry in every state in America.

▶ *The Complete Idiot's Guide to Wills and Estates* by Stephen M. Maple (Penguin Group USA, Penguin Group (USA) Inc., 405 Murray Hill Parkway, East Rutherford, NJ 07073; Telephone: 800-788-6262, http://www.penguinputnam.com). Lays out the whole process, including step-by-step directions for writing a will, language to be used in letters to executors and heirs, and power of attorney.

▶ *Estate Planning* by Martin M. Shenkman (Barron's Educational Series, 250 Wireless Blvd., Hauppage, NY 11788; Telephone: 631-434-3311; 800-645-3476; http://www.barronseduc.com). A guide to all the legal and tax aspects and financial details of estate planning.

Index

Notes